A CROWDED LONELINESS

by Debbie Shannon
with Bienvenida Catalina Miranda

*The story of loss, survival, and resilience
of a Peter Pan Child of Cuba*

This is a work of narrative non-fiction based on true events. Names, characters, and certain incidents are either memories told to me by Catalina or they are used fictitiously. I have made every effort to include historical facts wherever possible. I apologize for any historical errors.

Copyright © 2018 by Deborah Shannon
All rights reserved.

Library of Congress Control Number: 2018905017
ISBN: Hardcover 978-1-948981-04-0
ISBN: Paperback 978-1-948981-08-8
ISBN: Ebook 978-1-948981-09-5

Published in the United States of America

Book cover design by Robin Locke Monda
http://www.robinlockemonda.com/

Book interior design by David Provolo
https://reedsy.com/david-provolo

Photograph by Sharona Jacobs
http://www.sharonaphoto.com/

Second edition

Published by Fogbow Books, LLC, New York.
www.fogbowbooks.com

AUTHOR'S NOTE

I want to tell you how this book you are holding came into being. I met Catalina in New York City in 2006 shortly after I moved to Manhattan from Miami. We were both singing in a church choir at St. Joseph's Church on the Upper East Side. After mass, the choir often went to brunch together. I had lived in Miami for close to twenty years, so I was very familiar with the Cuban culture. I think that's one of the reasons why Catalina and I hit it off right away. We talked about Cuban food and the culture we both love.

At brunch one morning, Catalina mentioned that she was a Peter Pan kid. I was familiar with *Operación Pedro Pan* or Operation Peter Pan, which was the largest recorded exodus of unaccompanied children from Cuba in the Western Hemisphere. She told me that in 1961, her family decided to send Catalina, who was nine at the time, and her brother, Mario, who was eleven to the United States. They were first sent to Miami, and then a week later to separate orphanages in New Orleans. She and Mario, who are black, found themselves smack dab in the Jim Crow South.

She also told me how her family had been involved with Fidel Castro before and during the Cuban Revolution. Her brother, Lazaro, had even worked as Fidel's chauffer for a time. After Fidel came to power, however, he announced that he was a Communist. Her family felt betrayed by Fidel's shift in policy and became counter-revolutionaries.

"Catalina," I said, "if you're even a mediocre writer, you have to write your story."

"No. I want you to write it."

I was keen to take on the project. From a historical perspective, not many people outside Miami or Havana are familiar with Operation Peter Pan. There is another aspect of Catalina's story I found compelling. She told me that since her family was so involved in politics, the members of her family went their separate ways most of the time—drifting in and out of the house. Her father was seldom home. She said that she was surrounded by people but always felt alone. Later in New Orleans, she found herself again surrounded by people, but she felt isolated because she didn't fit in. She longed to be a part of a family and feel a sense of belonging. Hence the title *A Crowded Loneliness*.

Finally, with the Obama administration's warming of relations between the United States and Cuba, the Black Lives Matter Movement, and recent racial tensions, Catalina's story is as relevant today as it was in the 1960s. For these reasons, I really wanted to tell this story.

I interviewed Catalina once a week over the course of a year. Over lunch at my apartment, I recorded whatever experiences she could remember. She was in her early sixties at the time. Since this part of her story took place when she was between the ages of nine and thirteen, there were many instances where she just couldn't remember details, or the memories were too painful for her to recall. I used as much information as I could from Catalina, and then I diligently collected historical facts from other sources. I created the narrative arc by constructing scenes, dialogue, and in some cases names of people that Catalina had forgotten or simply couldn't communicate. Despite the historical correctness of the narrative, it is not a documentary, therefore, since parts of this story have been fictionalized, this story is considered narrative or creative non-fiction and not biography or memoir.

— Debbie Shannon

DEDICATION

This book is dedicated to the African American women of the United States. When my family wasn't there for me, they stepped in. In New Orleans, then later in Connecticut and New York, African American women were there to give me the support and encouragement that I needed.

I would like to thank Dr. Barbara Coulibaly. She was the one who encouraged me to write my story thirty years ago. After all these years, she is still in my corner.

I will be forever grateful to Sister Clement Marie, Mother Superior of the Orphanage St. John Berchman in New Orleans who took me under her wing. She guided me, nurtured me and protected me. As it turned out, we were kindred spirits.

Sister Clement Marie was also instrumental in introducing me to an utter angel, a woman whose name I don't even know. That woman brought me shopping each year to Maison Blanche, an upscale department store in New Orleans, for my Easter outfit complete with dress, shoes, socks, underwear, hat, pocketbook and gloves! She was generous and compassionate in every way. If that woman is still alive, I would love the opportunity to thank her personally.

My wish is to acknowledge these women in a very significant way. Although they never had riches, they all shared their love and bounty with me in abundance. They understood what I was going through first as a black child, then as a black teenager and later as an adult black woman. I share their struggle.

The Mammy figures have always been beloved, but black women in contemporary times, those who have been ignored, misunderstood, overlooked and disregarded, all share a special bond. I am proud to call them my sisters.

— Catalina Miranda, New York, NY

Chapter ONE

I'm sitting in my high-rise apartment on the Upper West Side of Manhattan sipping tea overlooking Lincoln Center. I often attend the opera or the ballet. All my favorite restaurants are within walking distance. I'm just a few blocks from Central Park. New York City is my home, and I feel very much a part of the city I love.

If someone had told me as a girl that I would one day be living in my very own high-rise apartment in Manhattan, I would have thought they were pulling my leg. You see, I wasn't born and raised in New York City. I was born in Cuba on the outskirts of Havana. When I was a girl a long time ago, the idea of leaving Cuba and living somewhere else seemed as impossible to me as flapping my arms and flying away. But it happened.

My journey to where I am now was not an easy one. In all my life, I have never told more than a handful of people my story—how I came to leave my country and how I ended up in New York City. Whenever I hear of those desperate people who die at sea on rafts trying to escape Cuba, I count my many blessings. You're probably wondering how I was able to leave. Pull up a chair and pour yourself some tea. This is how my story begins.

It was a hot summer evening, and I sat on the front porch watching a grey lizard fan its orange throat and listened to Radio Havana murmur deep inside the belly of the house, when the old man next door called me over. The only white men I knew were priests, and they were always good to me, so I had no reason to think that our neighbor, Mr. Molina, who I had never spoken to, was anything other than kind. I never saw this man during the day. He only came out at night.

The sidewalk was warm against my bare feet. I stepped up onto his cement porch and waited for him to say something. He sat alone in the dark corner, slouched in the wooden chair like an old pillow. He was a bald man with two bushy eyebrows that grew together over the bridge of his nose, which made him look like an egg with a misplaced mustache. He crossed his legs and rested an elbow on the arm of the chair and cradled his chin in the V of his thumb and index finger. He just looked at me. A buckle of noises from inside the house jangled out onto the porch: from a record player, the warm thrum of a guitar, the rhythmic clack of Claves and the deep donk of congas; the clatter of dinner dishes dealt like cards onto the table; his wife's off-key humming; laughter from his eight-year-old granddaughter, Esmeralda, who was my age.

Mr. Molina motioned to me with a nod, and I crossed the porch and stood beside him. He leaned toward me as if to tell me a secret. His hot breath was sour and moist against my neck. Before I knew what was happening, he reached up under my homemade cotton dress. He dug his weatherworn hand between my legs and into my panties. His finger scraped deep inside me.

"Supper is ready," his wife shouted.

He removed his hand from my panties, calmly stood and went inside. I ran home and told no one. My heart pounded so hard I thought I might pass out.

I thumped through our front door into the living room. My feet slapped against the cold ceramic tiles. The rooms in our house in Marianao, a southwest neighborhood of Havana, Cuba, were a series of four large rectangles, and in order to get from one room to the next, you had to pass through the previous room. I crossed the dark living room, sped through my parents' bedroom, then into the third rectangle which was divided down the middle by a narrow hallway. To the right was the bathroom, and to the left was a small bedroom that my sister, Lydia, and I shared. She was eight years older than me, and although I longed to be close to her, she ignored me. She made it clear that she didn't want anything to do with her baby sister. She had bigger fish to fry.

I ducked into my bedroom and swiped a fresh pair of panties from the dresser and darted across the hall into the bathroom. I eased the door shut, stripped off the old panties and scrubbed myself with soap and water.

"Caty, supper," my mother called from the kitchen. Her voice was low and smooth like molasses poured across the surface of polished wood.

"Sí, Mima."

I quickly dressed and headed toward the kitchen. The large, open room served as both cooking area and dining room. Dominating the right side of the room was a thick wooden table where we gathered to eat, elbow-to-elbow. There were eight of us, when everyone was home. On the left side of the kitchen, the refrigerator, sink, and cast-iron coal-burning stove huddled together. In the center of the stove sat a stone box where coal chunks glowed and puffed their hot breath up onto the burners. Mima stood at the stove with a spatula in her hand studying the plantain pucks and chunks of pork as they spit and bubbled in the frying pan. A white apron was knotted around her waist. She was statuesque with long limbs and elegant fingers. She had an exotic, Moorish look—coffee-colored skin, almond eyes, and long, kinky hair. I had inherited her complexion, hair, and tall frame.

I paused in the kitchen doorway to watch her move. Whereas I was reminded that I tore through the house like a small tornado, Mima never rushed. She took a step toward the refrigerator as if gliding across a ballroom dance floor, lifted the butter dish from the shelf, rotated, placed the dish on the table, and spun back toward the stove. The hem of her skirt swayed back and forth as though it had had too much to drink.

Lydia drifted through the front door and pushed her way past me into the kitchen. She snatched plates and silverware from the hutch beside the table. As I entered the kitchen, she glanced up briefly in my direction then turned away from me to set the table.

Lydia and I were never very close, but it wasn't just our age gap. I don't think we could have been more dissimilar if we had been born on different planets. She spent most of her days running the streets with romance on her mind. She was considered the black sheep of the family. They all dismissed her questionable behavior, hinting in whispered rumors that she "wasn't well." My mother had been pregnant with Lydia when her six-year-old son, Luis, died. My family assumed that the grief my mother had experienced seeped through the umbilical cord into her baby, and that this was why she had turned out wild.

Lydia knew how to wield the power of her shapely body to get the attention she craved. One day, the drunk in our neighborhood laid eyes on her. He approached my older brother Pete in the street in front of his friends and started to talk about her in a very suggestive manner. Pete came home in a rage and told my parents what was going on and how embarrassed he had been. That didn't stop Lydia. She danced to her own drumbeat. I haven't always agreed with her, but I admired that she lived her life on her terms, no matter what anyone else thought and regardless of the price she paid.

My brother Mario stumbled into the kitchen and flopped into a chair. Quiet and brooding, he was two years older than me. He had a cute baby face, which I had rarely seen coupled with a tall frame. We were oil and water. In my mind, a girl could do anything a boy could do. He was a macho, so in his mind, because he was a boy, he was better than me. That machismo attitude was backed up both at home and in our culture. Cuban mothers revered their sons. Education was important for all children, but parents especially encouraged their sons to excel personally, academically, and professionally. Daughters were expected to be smart, but mothers urged their girls to find a nice Cuban man to marry, cook Cuban food, and have lots of Cuban babies. Mima was no exception.

I stepped outside onto the cement patio just beyond the kitchen. To the left was a small area covered by a tin roof that sheltered a double sink and the big sack of coal we used for the stove. Two steps down beyond the patio, the back yard was surrounded by a seven-foot cement wall. I say it was a yard, but it was really more of a garden, because there was no grass. It was an area filled with dirt and plants. Mima grew everything—whatever she felt like growing, she grew.

Mima had gone to the country and brought back a little pink piglet. She wanted to raise him to slaughter for *Noche Buena*—Christmas Eve. There was a huge banana tree in the back on the left where the piglet roamed. He spent his days sprawled in the cool mud in the shade of the tree. That little thing made a lot of noise, but no more than our neighbors' chickens, roosters, and adult pigs.

We also had chickens and a rooster in a coop on the right toward the back of the garden. The hens hatched the cutest little fuzzy-yellow chicks you ever saw in your life. They looked so soft, I wanted desperately to touch them, but Mima said that if I did, I would get my smell on them, and the mother would reject them. In church during that time of year, the priest retold the story of how Jesus burst the bonds of Hell and walked out of the cave alive on the third day. I remember that the chicks broke free from their shells during Lent and Holy Week, so for me, I connect Lent and Holy Week with hatching chicks. Always have.

In the middle of the garden, Lydia scrubbed the laundry clean each Tuesday in a metal tub and a washboard. She flicked the wet clothes over lines that stretched from the tin roof to the back fence and hoisted them up away from the mud with long bamboo poles. After the laundry had baked dry in the afternoon sun, she lifted the clothing planks from the line and layered them in a basket for Mima to iron on Wednesday. Each day of the week, there were certain chores to be done. Mima skillfully governed our house like the captain of a tight ship, and because of her disciplined regiment, our home was always clean and organized.

I sat down on the warm cement and folded my legs under my dress. I heard the front door slam and turned and saw my older brothers Pete and George, who we called Nené, scuff across the kitchen. Nené kept his eyes focused on the floor and lowered himself slowly into a chair. Pete stood round-shouldered with his hands punched into his pockets and leaned his back against the wall.

Mima slid the frying pan off the burner and faced the boys. She crossed her arms across her chest as though she was cold although it was summer, and the kitchen was hot. I leaned my ear toward the door.

"Three more men were executed today," Pete said.

"The García brothers," Nené said.

"The Garcías who live near the church?" Mima asked.

"Yeah," Pete said. "Ché Guevara, Fidel Castro, and his brother Raúl found them holed up in a farmhouse outside Havana. They accused the men of treason because—"

"Because they talked about what Fidel was doing," Mima said.

Pete nodded. "They were led to a nearby forest. A priest had been driven out to the site to administer the last rites. They were allowed a final cigarette before being roped to a tree, blindfolded, and shot dead."

"Who told you this?" Lydia asked.

"The execution was filmed. We watched it live on TV."

It wasn't on our TV. We had been the first family in the neighborhood to own both a telephone and a television. In the evenings after dinner, our family gathered in the living room to watch TV together.

Fidel Castro had created an informant task force called the Committees for the Defense of the Revolution, or the CDR. Local CDR members were instructed to watch their neighbors' every move. They secretly kept detailed records of phone calls that people made, who visited whom and when these visits took place, people's work schedules, their education histories, and anything else that could be seen as "suspicious." No one was safe. Neighbors turned on neighbors. Brothers betrayed brothers. Anyone could report anyone, so at any moment, there was a real danger of being thrown in jail. Or worse. Disappeared.

The CDR pushed their way into people's homes under government orders and itemized the household possessions in order to nationalize all private property. They wanted to know exactly what you owned. Things that had been passed down in our family for generations became the property of the government. If anyone ever wanted to move to a different city or leave the country, the CDR would come in and take inventory. If that stuff wasn't there, you weren't allowed to go. All possessions had to be left behind and turned over to the government, or you needed to show the sales receipts and hand over the money. More important, having too many expensive items in the house made you a target. For that reason, our family decided to get rid of all big-ticket items that we could live without. That included our TV.

Mima listened to the boys without emotion. She turned back to the stove and scooped the plantains and pork onto a plate, then poured beans and rice into a bowl and set them on the table.

"Come on, let's eat," she said, sliding into a chair.

Instead, they all sat motionless and stared at the ribbons of steam rise from the food. They went on like that for a while, sitting together in silence. The cone of light from the overhead lamp cast eerie shadow masks on their faces. Mima's back was to me, and although I couldn't see her face, I could see her neck straighten and her head lift. Her spine stiffened under her dress, and her elegant presence hardened. I couldn't quite grasp the terror of what was happening, but I felt its weight. There was a heaviness to the air, a thickness you could feel. Like the tension in the atmosphere just before a storm hits.

I turned away from the door and hugged my knees to my chest and looked up at the simple shapes that the stars had pressed into the sky. I wanted so badly to fly away.

My father, who we all called Pipo, returned home late that night after I had gone to bed. He worked as a Merchant Marine. I didn't really know him well, because he was rarely home. He travelled for weeks at a time occasionally sailing to Mexico to do maneuvers, then home on leave for a day or two.

I woke to hear the mutter of voices in the kitchen despite the drone of Lydia's snoring. I pushed myself slowly from the bed and pressed my ear against the door. Pete was filling Pipo in on the executions.

"I heard about that," Pipo said. "The Garcías weren't the only ones. As soon as I left the ship, I overheard in the streets that several men had been rounded up and forced at gunpoint out to the cemetery. They were made to stand in line and wait their turn to die while they watched their friends' executions.

"This is madness," Mima said. "What are we going to do?"

"I don't know."

I felt safe with my brothers in the house, but whenever Pipo was home on leave, his presence afforded us all a sense of security. A shiver went through me. If Pipo didn't know what to do, who would?

The following afternoon, I found myself walking home alone from school and noticed that Mr. Molina was following me. As he approached me, I turned and stood my ground.

"Stop following me. If you don't stop bothering me, I will tell your wife."

He stood still for a moment with his mouth open in shock, then his unibrow lifted into a capital M. A smile slowly blossomed across his face. Without a word, he turned and walked away.

That evening, I ventured into our garden to pick vegetables for dinner and found that our piglet was dead. He had been poisoned. I find it hard to believe that he was killed because he made too much noise given the fact that just about everyone else kept animals that made plenty of noise on their own. Perhaps it had been a jealous Mrs. Molina. Mima once said that she resented the fact that we had a big back yard where we could grow things to sustain ourselves, and the Molinas had nothing but a stark cement slab. Mima pointed out that most people from the city looked down their noses at those who were raised in the country. Although I had been born and raised in the city, Mima was a country girl to the core, and she brought us up with a resourceful, resilient country mentality. Then again, it might have been something more. Maybe Mrs. Molina knew what her sick husband was up to.

In my heart, I suspected that it was in fact Mr. Molina who had poisoned our poor piglet as a form of payback for my rejection. I felt horrible that the little thing had to suffer because of something I had done. Regardless of who did it or why, it was a clear sign. The piglet's mouth foamed a warning.

Chapter TWO

A few days after the Garcías and the other men were murdered, Pipo was called back out to sea. I watched as Mima pressed and starched his uniform. Pipo was tall, dark, and lean, and when he stood in front of the mirror in his white uniform and black tie crisply knotted, he looked like a winning lottery ticket. He bent down for Mima to place the cap on his head and straighten it just so. The cherry on top.

Mima played music on the radio most of the time, and whenever Pipo was home on leave he would sing along. I would have loved to have heard Mima sing with that deep, lush voice of hers, but she never did.

And Pipo loved to dance. I remember watching him dance once in our living room at Lydia's *quinceañera*, her 15th birthday party. His spine swiveled and his arms and legs swayed like reeds in a gentle brook. His feet skimmed the floor as though he floated on air. He never danced with Mima, though. She wasn't interested. She was a simple, humble country girl whose life revolved around the three Cs—church, chores, and children. If she was able to go to daily Mass, complete her household chores and if her children were healthy, she was happy. She was plain, but in an elegant no fuss, no muss sort of way. She sewed herself pretty, fashionable outfits to wear, but she never spent time primping with her hair or painting her finger nails. On the rare occasions when she went out with Pipo, I would watch her tap red lipstick onto her lips in the bathroom mirror. She would then brush her lips with her fingertips and rub her dark brown cheeks into a rosy glow. She'd glance at me in the mirror and give me a wink. She looked just like a fresh stack of dollars.

Pipo may have danced with the ladies in the clubs, but he always came home to his wife and family. As far as I know, he never cheated on Mima, and we would have known. That town was way too small, and word would have gotten back to us if Pipo had fooled around. That said, I do remember one time when she threw him out of the house. I have no idea what he did to deserve his eviction, but I remember he got down on his knees and begged her to take him back. And she did.

For some reason, my father kept pictures of his old girlfriends in our family photo album. I can tell you, if that had been my husband, there would have been fireworks, but that didn't faze Mima in the least. In her mind, they were part of his past and not his present. He had chosen her, and that was all that mattered. I sometimes pulled the photo album from the drawer in their bedroom and flipped through the pages. I studied the faces of those young girls as they mugged for the camera in the years when Pipo was still deciding. Before Mima.

Any one of those girls could have been my mother, but I'm glad things worked out the way they did. I never questioned her love. Instead, I learned to accept her detached style as just the way things were. I know she loved us all deeply, but she either didn't know how to show it or was too afraid to let herself get emotional. In her world, especially at that time, when someone left the house, she couldn't be sure that they would return. She never took it for granted that life would be good. She assumed that life was always going to be a struggle.

We all loved each other in our own way, but our family seemed to be missing that special something that involved, nurturing parents give it. A sense of belonging. Of intimacy and sibling camaraderie. Of home. We weren't close-knit, but more like domino tiles scattered onto a table. It was every man and woman for themselves flowing in and out of the house doing our own thing. It was a crowded loneliness.

Each time just before Pipo left the house to go back out to sea, he circled his arms around Mima's waist and sang the old romance song by Roberto Cantoral García called *El Reloj* which means *The Clock*. That night, there was a lump-in-the-throat flutter to his voice as he sang about stopping the hands of time so the night would last, and the two of them could be together forever. He kissed her tenderly, but after a few seconds, she shook her head and waved him off with a smile. He adored that she wasn't the lovey-dovey type. She loved that he was. It was their dance.

He patted my head. "Be a good girl."

"I'll try."

He made his way to the front door, then stopped and turned back to Mima.

"I'll see you soon," he said.

"Yes, you will."

He nodded once and left. I followed him out the front door, stood on the porch, and leaned way over the cement railing to watch him walk away. I only caught a glimpse of him just before he disappeared into the black night.

My parents met while growing up in the westernmost province of the country called Pinar del Río. My mother, María de los Angeles Rodríguez Ezquivel, was born in 1910. She was the oldest child of Ernesto Ezquivel who was a dark-skinned black man and Angela Rodríguez who was part white and part Indian. All thirteen of their babies were exquisitely molded in every shade of mocha.

My grandfather owned a large tobacco farm. Just a few years earlier, Cuba had gained its independence from Spain, however, the few colonizers who remained had all but monopolized the tobacco trade. Their intention in staying behind in Cuba was to wipe out the rest of their competition.

One day, when my mother was ten years old, a group of Spaniards rode out to their farm on horseback. As they approached, my grandfather stepped outside and greeted them with a wave. My grandmother joined him and stood at his side. My mother remained inside the house and peered out from around the doorpost.

"We came to inform you that we are claiming this land in the name of Queen Isabella II," announced the leader.

"I won't let you do that. This is my land. Now, I'll have to ask you to leave at once."

Without another word, the man pulled out a gun and shot my grandfather. My grandmother collapsed onto her husband's lifeless body, wailing. My mother and the rest of the children burst from the house and flocked around their parents.

Instead of killing the rest of the family and claiming our land, the Spaniards turned and rode off. Perhaps they were moved at seeing the weeping children huddle over their dead father. For whatever reason, they never returned. My grandmother kept their land, but that offered her little consolation. They had robbed her of her beloved partner, and she fell into a deep depression. At ten, Mima became the primary caretaker, not only of her mother, but of the land, the home, and all her siblings.

Eight years later, she met my father, Aguedo (which is the masculine form of Agatha) Miranda Martínez. He was twenty-three and lived on a nearby farm. One afternoon, as she paused her work in the fields and stood to stretch her back, she spotted him strolling through their crops. She watched as he held his hands out at his side and caressed the tips of the tobacco leaves. He had the look of a man who didn't have a care in the world. As he sauntered closer, he smiled at her, and it was as though a cool breeze had caressed her face. His sweat-glistened skin shone like polished teak. Above all, it was his lightness of being that captured her heart.

The years caring for her mother and siblings had left her feeling serious, lonely, and hopeless, but what he saw in her was her strength of character, steadiness, and compassion—characteristics all the other girls he knew lacked. Her low, creamy voice was hypnotic to him. Because of his charm, he could have had any woman he wanted, but it was Mima who won his heart. By the end of the year, she had run away from her home and married Pipo in a quiet church service. They moved into a small wooden farmhouse with a thatched roof that his parents had built for them right next door to theirs.

Pipo worked as the manager of a nearby sugar mill. He was considered an educated man having gone to school up until the sixth grade, and for a black man at that time, that was remarkable. He managed his men well, but when racial tensions flared in the factory, Mima begged him to quit. She was terrified that he would be murdered by the hostile men just as her father had been murdered. Despite the death threats and her pleas for him to leave, he stayed on and was able to eventually win over his enemies and successfully manage the workers.

My parents didn't have children right away, but given Mima's complete devotion to her faith, I don't think that was by choice. I would imagine having a break from raising children would have been high on her to do list, but the Catholic Church not only taught but expected its followers to bring children into the world. The church was her all. I have a feeling she would have felt less "Catholic" if she hadn't obeyed. Four years into their marriage when Mima was twenty-three, she finally gave birth to their first child, Lazaro. Soon after he was born, she had her second child, a daughter, who sadly died shortly after her birth from some sort of heart condition. My father and mother were devastated by their loss.

They had their third child, Nené, then my brother Pete, then Luis, whose sweet personality I've been told was intoxicating. After the loss of their daughter, they made it a point to cherish the time they had with their children. Luis' favorite thing to do was to go to the beach, so the family often found themselves near the ocean every chance they could.

When Luis was 6 years old, he suddenly contracted typhus fever. They rushed him to the hospital, but because they lived way out in the country, it was too far away. They never made it in time. He died in my father's arms. The loss of their son was too much to bear. Joy vanished from the family as though a mean wind had burst uninvited into the house and snuffed out every bright candle. I was told that after Luis' death, Mima was never the same. Despite Pipo's coaxing, she no longer wanted to play with her children, and she shunned the beach.

If they had lived in the city, they believe Luis would have survived. So, they packed all their belongings and left their farmhouse to move into a dingy, one-room apartment in the back of a broken-down tenement house in Marianao. Pipo decided to enlist in the Merchant Marines. Eight years later, on March 22, 1953, I was born in the military hospital in Marianao.

For years, Mima talked about living in that one-room apartment as the best time of her life. I can't imagine why. That place was a dump. All eight of us were crammed together in that dark, damp, filthy room. There was a stove on one side where Mima cooked our meals, and a body-worn bed took up the other side of the room. Pipo was rarely home, so Mima and I slept together in the bed while the rest of the kids clustered on the floor. She kept a stinky chamber pot next to the foot of the bed, so anyone that needed to go in the middle of the night could do so in the pot. In the morning, she rinsed the revolting thing out and replaced it next to the bed.

Just outside the back door was a small courtyard surrounded by a wooden fence. It was just big enough to hold two small sheds. The courtyard smelled horrible because one of the sheds was a rickety old outhouse. Inside it was what looked like a wooden box with a hole knocked out of the top. A damp roll of toilet paper drooped against the wall in the corner. There was a crack in the wood along the mouth of the hole, so if you weren't careful, splinters latched themselves onto the back of your legs.

The second shed was a shower stall that consisted of a drainage hole in the middle of the floor surrounded by four empty clay walls that sweated in the clammy air. Instead of a warm, soothing shower from a sleek, polished faucet, cold water surged from a single rusty pipe that jutted from one of the walls. The force of the water was so excruciating that to avoid the torrent's assault, I darted in and out of the stream. One time, I happened to look up just as the water burst from the pipe. It shot up my nose, and I saw stars. I had a feeling that that was what it was like to drown in the ocean.

I remember during the summer rainy season when everything was weighted with moisture, I would stand quivering in the middle of the shower shed above the drainage hole as far away from the walls as humanly possible because fat earthworms poked out of that moist clay and slithered their way across the walls.

Four years later, we left that miserable apartment and moved to a slightly more tolerable three-room rental in the front of the same tenement house. As my brothers grew and became men, they finished school and brought money home for the family. Two years later, when I was six years old, we moved into our cement house with its four rectangle rooms and the walled garden. It was the last house I would ever know in Cuba.

Chapter THREE

The seeds of the Cuban Revolution had been planted in 1952, the year before I was born. Fulgencio Batista y Zaldivar, having successfully overthrown president Carlos Manuel de Céspedes on September 4, 1933 as part of the Sergeant's Revolt, realized he could once again return to power by running for president.[1]

In November 1939, Batista held elections for a constitutional convention which garnered him popularity with the masses. People from all parties and ideals would debate the best way to create a better Cuba for all. The 1940 Constitution promised great strides toward democracy in Cuba. Unfortunately, many of its principles were never implemented.[2]

Nevertheless, after twelve years of that new Constitution, Cuba was prospering. As the 1952 elections approached, three candidates ran for president: Carlos Hevia, an Annapolis graduate, Roberto Agramonte, and Batista. March 10, 1952 is an important day in Cuban history. As Election Day drew near, Batista saw the poles and knew that he was losing badly, so he cancelled the elections and seized control of the government in a second *coup d'état*. Batista destroyed the Constitution he himself had created. Even so, many welcomed Batista's return to power because it meant we were united with America. True to form, on March 27, 1952, the United States formally recognized Batista administration.[3]

Batista was corrupt through and through and soon made money hand-over-fist by partnering with the American mob.[4] Together they ruled the gambling, prostitution, and drug businesses in Havana. I heard Pete once say that at that time, marijuana and cocaine were as easy and as inexpensive to buy as a shot of rum. Our neighborhood teemed with casinos, brothels, and night clubs, particularly the famous Tropicana Club and the Buena Vista Social Club. Havana became an exotic, debaucherous retreat for the world's privileged class, and oh how the rich poured in to wallow.

Under Batista, a huge amount of the country's wealth was controlled by the sugar and tobacco barons, which left many people extremely poor. The little guy had had enough and was ready to rise up and fight. Fidel Alejandro Castro Ruiz, the illegitimate son of a wealthy farmer, wanted to create an agrarian society—a society based around producing and maintaining crops and farmland. My brothers agreed with his vision wholeheartedly.

Castro was an attorney and an up-and-coming politician who would have probably won a seat in Congress had those 1952 elections not been cancelled. So, for him, getting rid of Batista was personal. As soon as Batista took power, he began plotting to overthrow him. Almost all of Castro's early followers were lower middle-class or working-class young men. Many of them were from broken homes, or born out of wedlock like himself. They worked as parking lot attendants, street vendors, delivery boys, waiters, busboys, and chauffeurs.[5] Fidel admitted that he learned many of his guerrilla tactics from reading Ernest Hemingway's novel *For Whom the Bell Tolls* about combat used during the Spanish Civil War.[6] He steered clear of professionals and the educated, however, because they would have surely questioned his motives.

He began training his men within a few months, practicing at the University of Havana and at firing ranges. To avoid raising suspicion, his men came to the range dressed in business suits saying they wanted to learn how to shoot clay pigeons.

On the morning of July 26, 1953, Castro and his men made their move. They attacked the Moncada Barracks in Santiago de Cuba, because it was a military compound, and they would need ammunition and supplies if they were to go all the way with their plan. The raid was a complete failure, and the rebels were defeated handily within a few hours. Those who were not killed during the battle were either thrown into prison, or lined up and shot—just for spite.

At his trial, Castro openly accused Batista of committing barbaric acts against his own people. In order to shut him up, Batista had him separated from the rest of the prisoners and then lied to the courts saying that Fidel was too sick to attend the trials. Batista had no idea that he had sealed his own fate. Instead of testifying with the rest of the men, Castro was given his own personal trial in which he gave his famous four-hour speech called *History Will Absolve Me*. The resulting attention was just what he had hoped for. Once a nobody, he was suddenly basking in the limelight. He became the face of opposition, and his revolution acquired a name—*Movimiento 26 de Julio* or the July 26th Movement.

Despite the exhaustive speech, Castro and his men were found guilty and sentenced to fifteen years in prison.[7] International leaders and peace groups protested. Bowing to the pressure and to save face with the international community, within two years Batista had released all of the prisoners—including Fidel and Raúl.

Castro had no intention of giving up until Batista was either toppled from power or dead. He and Raúl fled to Mexico, where they met up with the Argentinian revolutionary named Ernesto "Ché" Guevara. In December 1956, Fidel, Raúl, and Ché led a group of eighty-two fighters to Cuba aboard a leaky old yacht named *Granma*, landing in the eastern part of the island. Batista's forces immediately killed or captured most of Castro's men. Fidel, Raúl, and Ché narrowly escaped, and with less than two dozen men, vanished into the Sierra Maestra Mountains. There they established their base camp, and with the help of the local peasant sympathizers, they laid out their plans for the revolution.[8]

In an attempt to retain control of his power, to terrorize, and to make it perfectly clear to the Cuban people he would not stand for an uprising, Batista's police were ordered to torture and kill young men in the cities who were suspected of insurrection. Many innocent people, including small children, were publicly executed as a warning to anyone who considered joining the rebellion. Hundreds of slaughtered bodies dangled from lamp posts for days or were dumped in the streets like trash.[9] There was no partiality when it came to the firing squad. Black and white, rich and poor, young and old—all stood shoulder to shoulder against the wall. When the bullets were fired, they all slumped to the dirt in a bloody heap. It's thought that up to twenty thousand souls were murdered by Batista's men.[10]

That brutal behavior backfired. People had become repulsed by Batista and his savage reign. Castro, who had been backed by just a few in the beginning, soon found himself supported by the influential middle and upper class: doctors, lawyers, and bankers. Finally, after a decade of developing his political philosophy and plotting his revolution, Fidel's time had come. My brother, Lazaro, left Havana and traveled to the mountains in order to fight with him. I don't know exactly what all of his duties were, but I heard he served as Castro's personal chauffeur.

The Cuban Revolution was a patriotic movement in order to liberate Cuba's people and to fight corruption. It was never a Communist Revolution. While Castro's small group of guerrillas were in the mountains, rebels in the cities, among them my brothers, set off homemade fire bombs in different locations throughout Havana. The city was without water for three days, and the airport was completely gutted by fire. Buses in cities and on highways, trucks carrying freight and merchandise, passenger trains, railroad and highway bridges, public buildings, homes, and businesses were blown up or burned. The rebels succeeded in keeping things in a constant state of turmoil.

On New Year's Eve, 1958, Batista realized that his presidency was over. After celebrating the New Year at a festive party, he gathered a small group of his closest political and military friends, loaded about six airplanes, and at 3:00 a.m., fled the country to the Dominican Republic. In the days that followed, people gathered in the streets and cheered the rebels as they streamed into town in trucks coming down from the mountains.[11]

It took several days for Castro to make his way to Havana. He drove across the country, and along the way, rallied seas of jubilant people.

By the time that he rode victoriously into Havana on January ninth, a million people were in the streets.

I remember watching it on TV like it was yesterday. The neighborhood outside our house was like a ghost town, because everyone went to the center of Havana to be a part of the celebration. They believed the victory was not only Fidel's, but their victory as well. Horns blared. The black and red flag of the July 26th Movement waved from cars and fluttered from windows against the buildings. I have always loved the color combination of red and black and often wear these colors. To me, they represent hope, idealism, and the spirit of freedom. We had dreamed of a better life. Crowds of euphoric people danced in the streets, and we danced with them in our living room.

We all wanted to hear what Fidel had to say. As he was making his victory speech, several white doves appeared and rested upon his shoulder, arm, and the podium. Cubans are very superstitious, and if you know anything about Santería, you'd know that a white dove is a very symbolic animal. It was an immediate sign to everyone that Fidel had been blessed by the Santería saint. The white doves meant he had been chosen to be our deliverer. Fidel was the one to liberate Cuba from its bonds and carry it into a peaceful, prosperous future.[12]

We listened to Fidel speak, and we exalted him. We were finally free and out from under Batista's heel. As we rejoiced, we had no idea we were celebrating the very thing that would lead to our downfall.

Chapter **FOUR**

My parents wanted to live in a more elegant neighborhood. Our house was comfortable, but Mima longed to live in a big beautiful house with lots of land. She volunteered at La Santa Cruz Catholic Church on the other side of town polishing the pews, organizing, ordering the supplies, and pressing the altar linens. She liked being in that area of town. The houses there were what we would consider mansions. She took her time coming home each day, walking through the neighborhood and admiring the houses and landscaping.

One afternoon, she happened to recognize one of the parishioners on her front lawn, so she waved to her. The woman waved back and motioned for her to come over.

"I know you from the church," the woman said.

"Yes. I was just on my way home and was admiring your house. One day, I'd like to buy a house in this neighborhood, too."

"Oh, you wouldn't like living here."

"Why not?"

"I'm just not sure you and your family would fit in."

"I see," Mima said. "Well, enjoy your day."

She walked away from the woman knowing exactly what was meant by us not fitting in. There was no doubt in her mind that we wouldn't fit in, according to that woman, because we were black, and that neighborhood was white. By and large, people of all races and skin shades worked and lived together in peace and with respect. There were instances like this, however, where elitists bluntly put you right in your place.

That racist dig didn't deter Mima. She never gave up and eventually found the perfect plot of land just outside of town where she could build her dream home. She took the money she had scrimped and saved from my father and brothers for years and finally bought her land.

By the end of 1960, Castro had nationalized more than $25 billion worth of private property owned by Cubans including all foreign-owned property. That meant that farms of every size were seized, and all land, businesses, and companies owned by upper- and middle-class Cubans were nationalized, even the plantations owned by Castro's own family. Shortly after Mima bought her prized land, Castro confiscated it, unspooling her dream. She would never see her beautiful home realized. After all those years of sacrificing, it was gone with the wave of a hand. The loss was immense. She fell into a deep depression and didn't leave her bed for a month.

Just after her land was stolen from her, Mima's brother, Catalino Ezquivel, was committed to an insane asylum, even though he wasn't crazy in the least. He was angered by all that Fidel was doing and told his friends and neighbors how he felt. They all warned him to be quiet, but he continued to criticize Castro's actions, so the government had him committed against his will. After a month, one of the asylum workers came to the house. I stood in Mima's bedroom, peering into the living room as she answered the door. The man remained on the porch and removed his hat.

"I'm sorry to inform you that your brother, Catalino, is dead."

Mima tried to steady herself against the wall, but fell to the floor. The man dropped his hat and came in and helped her to her feet. He guided her into a chair.

"Can I get you anything?" he asked.

"They killed him. He didn't just die. They killed him, and you know I'm right."

The man flicked his eyes to the floor. "I'm sorry for your loss." He stood, picked up his hat, and closed the front door behind him.

Once in power, Fidel quickly swept away any shred of Batista's government and at the same time squashed any lingering rebel cells. Raúl Castro and Ché Guevara were put in charge of bringing suspects under the old regime to trial for their "war crimes."

Ernesto "Ché" Guevara has become a popular cultural icon. His face adorns posters, building murals, and T-shirts around the globe, and he was even glorified in the popular movie *The Motorcycle Diaries*. It makes my blood boil to see him revered. I'm sure those who flaunt his likeness have no idea the kind of monster this man was. They don't realize that he was Fidel's chief enforcer, and that he was in charge of at least one hundred deaths by firing squad—in many cases picking up the gun and firing the fatal shot himself.

Ché was quoted as saying, "Crazy with fury I will stain my rifle red while slaughtering any enemy that falls in my hands! My nostrils dilate while savoring the acrid odor of gunpowder and blood. With the deaths of my enemies I prepare my being for the sacred fight and join the triumphant proletariat with a bestial howl!

He continued, "Hatred as an element of struggle; unbending hatred for the enemy, which pushes a human being beyond his natural limitations, making him into an effective, violent, selective, and cold-blooded killing machine. This is what our soldiers must become…"[13]

In his book *Exposing the Real Che Guevara: And the Useful Idiots Who Idolize Him*, Humberto Fontova quotes Ché as saying, "To send men to the firing squad, judicial proof is unnecessary. These procedures are an archaic bourgeois detail. This is a revolution. And a revolutionary must become a cold killing machine motivated by pure hate."[14]

In 1964, Guevara addressed the UN General Assembly. "Executions? We execute! And we will continue executing as long as it is necessary."[15] Make no mistake. That man is not to be idolized. He was truly a cold-blooded killing machine.

Pipo was forced to resign his position in the Marines. He loved his job and had served his country faithfully, but in Fidel's eyes, anyone who worked under Batista was considered to be "on his side." He was lucky he wasn't thrown in jail or executed. Instead, he came home to us, but he was never the same. Being labeled a traitor broke him. All those years, he defended our country with pride. He sacrificed his time with his family to work hard so we could have whatever we needed. He tried to at least collect his pension, but the government refused him that as well.

In an attempt to clean house, Castro immediately closed the casinos and night clubs, among them the Buena Vista Social Club—Pipo's favorite hangout. With the exception of his family, everything that had fulfilled him and had given him pleasure in his life was gone. I watched the happiness drain from him like water from a cracked pot. He no longer sang to the radio or danced around the house. He sat in his chair and stared at the living room floor, or he would stand and pace back and forth and lash out at anyone who came near him. My heart bled for him, but I didn't know how to tell him how sorry I was that he was unhappy, so I left him alone.

Pete came home early from seminary one afternoon wearing his street clothes. He scuffled through the house straight to the kitchen and poured himself a glass of water. Mima stood at the stove and pushed a wooden spoon around in a pot of black beans. I sat at the dining room table playing with Cubilete dice. Mima and I watched Pete as he took a long drink, then stared at the floor.

"Why aren't you in class?" Mima asked. "Where's your cassock?"

He just shook his head.

"What happened?"

He said nothing. He took another drink and went outside on the patio and stood there for a long time with one hand on his hip just looking up at the sky. Pete was solid and steady. He was my father figure and the man of the house while Pipo was away. He was tall, dark, and lean like Pipo and had charisma by the bucketful. He glowed from within as though he had swallowed sunlight. I was frightened to see him so unsettled. Mima and I waited for him to say something.

"It's over. The seminary is closed."

"What do you mean?" Mima asked stepping out onto the patio.

"Castro closed it, and soon the Catholic schools and churches will be closed, too. There was an announcement that he will nationalize all property held by the church. Hundreds of priests are to be expelled from the country."

"Oh, my God," she said.

"Castro declared that Cuba is now officially atheist and that he is a communist. A communist! I wouldn't be surprised if that was his plan all along."

"What does this mean?"

"It means that if you're a communist, you can't be Catholic."

Mima stood with her arms at her side looking up at the clouds. Imagine, here was a woman who went to church every single day no matter the weather and prayed the rosary every night. Pete studied years to become a priest. That's how entrenched my family was in the Catholic Church. Not being Catholic was simply unthinkable.

"It's not just the Catholics. All private schools are banned now, too. There will only be government-run schools. They say some children will be sent away to study on collective farms in the Soviet Union."

"No one is taking my children anywhere."

"Agree." Pete took another long drink. "We all put our lives on the line for that guy—for the Revolution. And he lied to us. I'll tell you this, I'm going to do everything I can to get rid of that bastard."

"What do you have in mind?"

Pete turned toward her and smiled. "Chaos."

Chapter **FIVE**

"Caty, get up." Mima burst into my room and threw the covers off my body. "You're coming to church with me."

"Why?"

"Because if I leave you alone, by the time I got back, the house would be destroyed."

Mario and I were home throughout the day. After the Catholic school closed, Mima made arrangements for Mario and me to be tutored privately at the one-room schoolhouse nearby, but we weren't there long. She realized it wasn't safe. We were breaking the law because we weren't attending the government-run schools. The neighborhood watchdogs could turn us in, so she quietly withdrew us.

I wiggled into my dress and joined her in the kitchen. Mima poured me a glass of milk while I buttered warm bread. After sucking my fingers clean, I washed up, and we headed for church. People were either off to work early or still inside when we left the house, so it was somewhat safe for me to be seen with her at that time of day.

Most days we attended daily Mass at La Santa Cruz, but sometimes, we walked an hour to attend mass at St. Francis of Assisi Church. It was nestled in a cove beside the beach. As we approached the shore, the cool sea breeze misted my hair and my face. I could smell the salt in the air. I never asked to go onto the beach, though. It wasn't something my family ever did, so it never occurred to me to want to go near the water. Still, I gazed at the blue-grey sea beyond the seawall as we drifted along the walkway. The motion of the waves soothed me. It was hypnotic, like the soft flicker of a flame.

It's nice when you can be friendly with your mother, but Mima and I weren't close. I could never talk to her about silly things let alone anything serious. She wasn't mean at all, just sober. She seemed chattier with the boys. Maybe it was because when they were young, she was still healthy. By the time I came along, the woman I knew was plagued with asthma attacks and frequent bouts of depression from her bipolar disorder. She was down more than up.

To be alone with her for an extended period of time was rare. On those tender mornings on the road to St. Francis, we walked hand-and-hand together without speaking. Words weren't needed. She had me, and I had her. It was as though I was her only child.

We entered the front door and made our way to the right-hand side of the church. We always sat in the front on the right side. I remember attending a wedding once and our family was seated on the left-hand side. I couldn't concentrate on what the priest said, because everything felt out of place. When I was on the right side, everything was in order.

The church was beautiful in its simplicity. A series of round stone columns stood sentinel over the congregation and rose up to meet at the domed ceiling. Candlelight glowed against the marble walls in creamy shades of beige, grey, and white. It was cool, quiet, and welcoming. As soon as we entered, I felt protected. During the Mass, as we prayed and sang, and the everyday rituals soothed me like soft warm waves.

I remember during one of my last visits to St. Francis, we sat quietly in the back and watched a wedding that was taking place. I rolled the church bulletin into a telescope and leaned under the pew to peep at the stockinged ankles in fancy high heels. That afternoon for some reason, the statues glowed with the candlelight. Sunbeams poured in through the stained-glass windows onto shoulders and hats and the just-married couple who knelt before the priest, heads bowed, peeking at each other under the mantilla. It was as though God had cupped us all safely in His palm.

Once we left the sanctuary of the church, we walked straight home. We kept our eyes focused on the ground and tried not to call attention to ourselves. As soon as Mima and I arrived, she shut and locked the front door behind us and went straight to the back of the house to start her chores. Mario and I weren't allowed to go anywhere without her, and we certainly weren't allowed outside during the day. We couldn't risk the neighbors seeing us. My childhood became a lonely clutter of days spent behind locked doors. I was consumed with the dread of being imprisoned in that house for the rest of my life. I couldn't see the future.

I woke that night to the sound of screaming outside my bedroom window. It was late at night, and the next-door neighbors were in their front yard fighting with the police who had come to arrest Lazaro. Since our neighbor's son was also named Lazaro, they raided the wrong house and arrested the wrong man.

Regrettably, the police eventually found and arrested my brother. He and his fellow counterrevolutionaries had been holed up in a house on the edge of town. He was sentenced to 30 years in prison, which was a blessing of sorts. Since Lazaro had worked so closely with Fidel during the Revolution, his betrayal made him the worst sort of traitor. Others like him were shot right on the spot. Yes, he was in jail, but he was still alive.

Pipo borrowed a neighbor's car so we could visit him. We drove south about an hour to the coast and boarded a ferry. He was being held in the prison called *Presidio Modelo* or the Model Prison on what was then called the *Isla de Pinos* or the Isle of Pines. It's now known as *Isla de la Juventud* or the Isle of Youth. During Spanish colonial times, the island had been used as a penal colony.

The Model Prison was made up of four massive circular six-story buildings. In 1926, the dictator, Gerardo Machado, was so impressed by the notorious panoptic Stateville Correctional Center in Joliet, IL in the U.S., he commissioned the Model Prison to be built by its future inmates as an exact replica.[16]

The concept of the panopticon layout is that there is a central tower surrounded by prison cells. Think of a silo on a farm with all the cells along the inner circumference of the walls. The tower sits in the middle of the silo where the watchman (-opticon) can observer all the prisoners (pan-) in their cells at the same time.[17]

We parked the car and were escorted to a room where guards searched all of us. We were then asked to wait in a large, open room with long wooden tables and metal folding chairs that scraped and squeaked. When Lazaro entered the visitor's area, he appeared calm as if he had come to terms with his fate. He was short and had always been muscular, but I could see he had already lost weight. He said hello to me and Mario, but then the two of us sat quietly off to the side while he spoke with my parents and brothers. They sat across from Lazaro at the table. Pipo reached out and held his hand. The prison guard at the door glared at Pipo and took a step forward. Pipo calmly glanced at the guard, but never released Lazaro's hand. The guard paused, then took a step back.

"Quite a place you got here," Pipo whispered, trying to diffuse the tension.

"Yeah, a regular Shangri-La."

"This is a ridiculous question, but how are you holding up?" Nené asked.

Lazaro shook his head. "They pack us in two or three to a cell. There's a brick wall on the right and left side of the cell, but the back is made of glass, so we're backlit. We're constantly observed from the guard tower. There's zero privacy."

Lazaro let out a long sigh. "It's not just those fighting Castro who are in here," he said. "He's rounded up homosexuals, Jehovah's Witnesses, and anyone else he considers virulent. I heard there are anywhere from 6,000 to 8,000 of us in here. Like rats in a granary. Ironically, Castro and his men were sent here, too, after his attack on Moncada."

Lazaro paused. The guard left his post at the door and slowly paced behind him, as if we needed to be reminded of his presence, then made his way back to the door and stood at attention. Lazaro leaned in closer.

"The tower constantly shines a bright light into the cells, so the guards can see us but we can't see them. It's an interesting form of psychological torture."

"How do you sleep?" Mima asked.

"We rip small pieces of cloth from our trousers and place them over our eyes at night. Speaking of psychological torture, we watched workers drill holes under the ground floor of the prison and fill them with dynamite. It can be ignited from far away with a battery. They threaten to blow us sky high at any moment, supposedly to keep us from staging a prison break. So, there's that."

He licked a finger and rubbed dried blood from a knuckle.

"They work us hard. Some guys refused. The bastard sergeant took the butt of his rifle and pounded one of them in the head. He went down like a sack of potatoes, but the guy kept beating him. One was taken out into the field and thrashed with the blade of a bayonet until his bloody hip bone poked out of his skin."

"Jesus," Pete said. "Something has to be done."

Lazaro shrugged. "I can tell you a hundred stories like that."

"I'm terrified something like that will happen to you." Mima said.

"Don't worry about me. I'll keep my head down."

"Times up," the guard said. "Say your goodbyes."

We hugged and kissed him, and then the guard escorted him through the door back to his cell. We all stood and watched the door slowly slide shut and listened to the loud clank of the lock. We shuffled back to the car, boarded the ferry, and drove home in silence.

Since Pipo was no longer allowed to work, Pete and Nené toiled all hours to put food on the table. One evening while we sat down to dinner, I noticed Pete wasn't there.

"Where's Pete?" I asked.

"He's not coming," Pipo said. "He went underground. He's in hiding."

"He's hiding in the dirt?"

"No, that means he's in a secret location."

"Lazaro was in a secret location."

"Yes, he was."

"So, the police can find this location."

"We hope they won't," Mima said, "but yes, they can."

Later that night, I went to bed, but I couldn't sleep. I remember staring at the ceiling as though I could look right through it up to heaven, and I prayed for Pete. I asked God to keep him safe, wherever he was, and to keep him hidden.

Chapter **SIX**

One afternoon, Pipo decided to fix something on the patio. I wanted to help, so I hovered nearby in the kitchen. For some reason, he had placed the hammer that he was using head-side first onto the hot stove. I picked it up, and the hot metal burned my hand. I dropped it on the floor, and his eyes narrowed.

"What did you go and do a stupid thing like that for?"

"I don't know."

His tight face softened, and his eyes grew sorrowful. He looked directly at me, then through me as though focused on some imaginary point in the distance. He looked tired. Wrinkles roadmapped his face, and he wore his skin loose like an old sweater that had been stretched. He was a stranger in the present tense.

The expression to get "choked up" is so appropriate, because that's exactly what happened. My heart swelled, and my throat seized up. There were so many things I wanted to tell him—that I was sorry I got in his way, that I understood that he was frustrated, that I wished things were better for him, that I loved him—but I couldn't speak. Instead, I ran to the bathroom and held my palm under the cold water then fled to my room.

A while later, Pipo popped his head through the bedroom door. I looked up from my doll.

"I'll be back. I'm just going to pick up some bread at the bakery."

Not long after that, I heard banging on the front door. I ran to answer it, but a man I recognized from the neighborhood pushed past me through the door and into our living room.

"María," he shouted.

Mima came running from the kitchen.

"Aguedo fell in the bakery."

"What happened?"

"I don't know. They've taken him to the hospital. I'll come back with a car to take you there."

She nodded and then turned toward me. "Get your shoes on."

The neighbor dropped Mima, Mario, and me off at the hospital entrance. We followed a nurse whose shoe squeaks echoed down a long white hall. She led us to a room and motioned for us to go inside. Pipo was asleep in the bed and hooked up to a ventilator. Somehow, someone had contacted Nené, Lydia, and Pete, because they were already there with the doctor.

"What happened?" Mima asked.

"He had a massive stroke," the doctor said.

"He'll wake up, though, won't he?"

The doctor touched her elbow. "It's not good."

We spent the rest of the week at Pipo's side. Nurses, smelling of soap, softly skimmed their carts in and out of the room, checked his vitals, and whispered to us their sympathetic can-I-get-you-somethings then backed out as though the queen were present. Some of us prayed, others sat bewildered and watched his chest rise and fall with the cottony whoosh of the breathing machine. Mima clung to Pipo's hand, their fingers wound like vines.

By the end of the week, he had contracted pneumonia, and on January 19, 1962, he breathed his last. He was forty-eight years old. His death was peaceful, and we were all quiet in our mourning. There was no crying or screeching or carrying on. It was just heartsore acceptance.

I overheard a few people say "He had a good life." How many years constitutes a good life? There were so many things Pipo didn't get a chance to do—or places he and Mima would never visit. All those plans tossed in the trash. He would never walk me down the aisle or know my children. To farm again, something he loved to do. To listen to more baseball games on the radio. To dance, oh to dance. And all those love songs left unsung.

Is it better to know when a person is in the process of dying, like say those fighting cancer, so that you have time to say what you need to say? Or is it better when the person is taken from you quickly, without goodbyes and I love yous? I don't know the answer, but I have a feeling neither is good. No matter how much time you have before someone you love dearly is taken, there is never enough time. There are never enough words.

Cuban funerals are performed within twenty-four hours of someone's death, not necessarily out of any religious custom, but because at that time, they didn't embalm the bodies, and the tropical heat claimed the remains right away.

A Cuban wake is an all-night affair. The body is either taken to the family's home and set up in the living room or taken to a funeral home. Pete made arrangements for Pipo to be taken to a nearby funeral home. When we arrived, Pipo was already resting in a casket in the front of a softly lit room. Folding chairs were placed in neat rows like church pews. White flower arrangements stood at his head and feet.

The casket was closed, although there was a glass window in the lid so that the body could be seen but not touched. Some believe that a dead body is surrounded by a negatively charged aura that is a conduit for ghosts, demons, and evil spirits. By kissing or touching the dead in this corrupted state, that person could unwillingly allow those negative energies to enter their own body.

During the wake, the body is never to be left alone. Most people don't eat, although they might have espresso with milk and some bread, but that's it. Those who do step out, do so in shifts. We all stayed awake throughout the night in order to keep Pipo company.

Cubans tend to be loud—not with crying or wailing, but with the sound of their voices. They talk up and over each other instead of lowering their volume or whispering as though in church. By midnight that night, it was a vocal free-for-all. Neighbors, friends, and relatives came and reminisced about Pipo's dancing, his jokes, and his smile. They slap-back laughed, shook their heads, and wiped tears. I sat off to the side and made paper flowers with the tissues.

In the morning, the funeral home director entered the room and stood beside Pipo.

"It's now time to proceed to the cemetery. The funeral will be held at 11:00 a.m."

As everyone gathered their things to leave, Mima leaned over me.

"Caty, I want you to go home, now. Mrs. Cosío will take you and stay with you until we get back."

I was so tired that I didn't put up a fight. While the rest funneled out the front, our neighbor, Mrs. Cosío, and I ducked out the side door. As soon as I got home, I climbed into my PJs, slipped into bed, and fell fast asleep.

Love is stronger than death. It doesn't perish, instead it lingers, as when an astronaut wrings water from a rag, it floats nearby then drifts on, but stays close. Having love without a body so near doesn't always soothe. After Pipo's death, Mima changed. After she came home from the cemetery, she staggered to her bedroom and shut herself in. Our lives had always been hijacked by her bouts of depressions, but this was exceptional. Weeks passed. She donned a black dress, remained in her room, and stopped communicating—not so much as a "Caty, can you get me a glass of water?" or "Cook me a piece of fish." Nothing. She stopped going to mass and doing her daily chores. She made us draw all the shades in the house, casting us all into the darkness with her.

Our house had been forlorn and dreary all winter. Seemingly overnight, the winds shifted and the weather grew warm. Spring was finally in the air. One morning, I got out of bed and turned on some music. I grabbed the broom and started the spring cleaning. I was in the living room and had paused my sweeping for a moment to dance with the broom. Wouldn't you know it, my grandmother, Pipo's mother, who never ever visited us, decided to stop by. She plowed through the front door and stormed toward me. She was short and delicate looking, but the fires of hell flashed in her wide eyes.

"What do you think you're doing?" She slapped off the radio.

"I'm cleaning."

"Your father is dead. You're supposed to be in mourning for a year."

I quickly put the broom away and ran to my room and stayed there until she left.

Chapter SEVEN

"Come outside and sit with me, Caty" Nené said.

He led me out to the front porch and settled himself beside me. Whereas Pete was the father figure in our house, Nené was our mother hen, and he took good care of his little chicks—even Mima. He was the one who shepherded her through her many ups and downs. That man had the patience of Job.

"I have something important to tell you," he said. "You and Mario have to go away for a while. The Catholic Church in Miami is going to arrange for us all to get out of Cuba. They are helping the children escape first, and then we will soon follow and meet up with you both there.

I found out later that before Pipo's stroke, despite the danger and uncertainty, he, Mima, and my brothers had agreed that Mario and I should be sent to the United States. *Operación Pedro Pan* or Operation Peter Pan officially launched in 1960. Its name came from J.M. Barrie's story of *Peter Pan* who took three children with him to Never-Neverland. The idea of this rescue mission was developed by Father Bryan O. Walsh, director of the Catholic Welfare Bureau in Miami, Fl. He partnered with the U.S. State Department to issue official visas from 1960 to 1962 to Cuban children between the ages of five and eighteen—only the children, not their parents. Desperate and frightened for their children's future under Castro, parents trusted the Catholic Church. They placed over 14,000 unaccompanied children on airplanes bound for Miami with the hope that they, too, might join them one day.[18]

The idea of transporting children to safety during times of political upheaval or war wasn't new. After the Nazis' violent pogrom *Kristallnacht* or Night of Broken Glass against the Jews on November 9-10, 1938, the British authorities agreed to rescue thousands of Jewish children from Germany, Austria, Czechoslovakia, and Poland by granting them official travel visas. It was understood that those children, who were not accompanied by their parents, would eventually return to their families. Private citizens offered to pay for each child's care until the crisis was over. In all, the rescue operation, dubbed *Kindertransport,* brought about 7,500 Jewish children to Great Britain. Unfortunately, because the majority of their parents were murdered during the Holocaust, most of these children never saw their families again. Many of them became citizens of Great Britain, or emigrated to Israel, the United States, Australia, and Canada.[19]

Shortly after the British government rescued those *Kindertransport* children, they were faced with the gut-wrenching decision to relocate their own children to safety. During the summer of 1939, as war appeared imminent, the government decided to evacuate almost three million people, most of them children, from high-risk cities and shipped them to rural areas in Britain as well as overseas to Canada, South Africa, Australia, New Zealand, and the United States. Operation Pied Piper was the biggest and most concentrated population movement in British history.[20]

In many cases, civic officials in rural counties corralled the newly arrived children and lined them up against a village wall or up on a stage for the prospective host families to take their pick. Often, the phrase "I'll take that one" haunted those poor children for the rest of their lives. There were so many children from different backgrounds and social classes, and their experiences with their host families ranged from pleasant to horrific. Allowing perfect strangers, without any kind of background check, to take in these vulnerable children was very risky and every pedophile's dream.[21]

Operation Pied Piper influenced future works of literature. C.S. Lewis drew inspiration from June Flewett, a famous actress and stage director now named Jill Freud, but then a young London convent girl and one of many children who stayed with him during the air raids on London. In his novel *The Lion, the Witch and the Wardrobe,* Peter, Susan, Edmund, and Lucy Pevensie are sent from London to a country manor where they find a portal in a wardrobe full of fur coats into the snowflakes of Narnia.[22] *The Lord of the Flies* by William Golding is about a plane filled with evacuated boys shot down over a tropical island. After watching newsreels of the evacuated children with notes pinned to their clothing and looped around their necks, Michael Bond wrote *Paddington Bear* about an orphaned bear found at Paddington Station in London sitting on his suitcase with a note attached to his coat that read "Please look after this bear. Thank you."

As for Operation Peter Pan, if Mario and I were to take part, Mima had to get us out of the country quickly, because the deadline was fast approaching. One thing was perfectly clear to her. If her children remained in Cuba, we'd either be sent to the Soviet Union to serve in work camps or trapped on the communist island and never get out.

"Where will we go?" I asked.

"They'll have a nice place for you there in Miami."

"Like an orphanage?"

"No, you won't be in an orphanage. The Church will take good care of you. You and Mario will leave next week. We'll all be together there soon. Don't be afraid or sad."

Thinking back, I wasn't afraid or sad. Sorrows had come to our family in stampedes. Lazaro was in jail, my father lost his job, his will to live, and his very life, and Pete fled underground somewhere to avoid being captured or killed. I understood all too well the evils of communism.

What I remember most about my time in Cuba was a never-ending conflict that thickened the air and latched itself onto us like an unholy shadow. It had shaped our lives in so many unfortunate ways. Our family had an opportunity to leave Cuba, and I was excited to go. I thought, like Peter Pan, we were really going to Never-Neverland. I knew we were going to America, and that's just how I pictured it to be. My family had suffered terribly, and I had been locked up in that house for so long. Leaving Cuba meant that we would be free from the turmoil. It would be a new beginning.

The government gave us a list of things that we were allowed to pack—pajamas, slippers, and a change of clothing, nothing more. Mario and I shared a small suitcase. We weren't allowed to take any money, or pictures, or toys. I had no idea what Mima had packed for me, but it didn't matter.

On the morning that we were supposed to leave, I took a long, hot shower. I scraped the bar of soap across a bath brush and scrubbed my body to where it nearly shined and then let the water pound my tingling body. I pulled the steam into my lungs and felt my body expand. For the first time in my life, I felt independent. I was about to go to America. Of course, because Lydia was much older, she could do almost anything I couldn't do. This was the first time that I was going to do something she hadn't done.

After my shower, I went to my room to dress. I saw that Mima had laid out a beautiful new dress for me to wear. I had no idea she had made it for me. It was white with delicate pleats and a silky blue belt. My nickname "CATY" had been embroidered on the back in light blue thread—the colors of the Virgin. I pulled the new dress over my head and looked for Mima to show her, but she was nowhere to be found.

"Caty, come here," Nené called from the living room. "I have a surprise for you."

I entered the room and fashion-model spun for him.

"You look beautiful."

"Thank you. What's the surprise?"

"Mima asked me to take you to the hair salon to get your hair done."

My hair is naturally nappy, but Mima tamed it every morning by patiently combing and braiding for me. I followed him down the street to the nearby hair salon, where a chubby, black woman was waiting for me. Her shoulder-length hair had been pulled straight back and flipped up at the ends. Where her eyebrows had once been, two thin black lines of eyebrow pencil umbrellaed her large brown eyes. I sat in the chair and let her pull and smooth my hair into two glossy braids.

With my hair professionally done and my new dress on, I felt beautiful. After we came home, Nené and Mario stayed outside on the porch and talked. I took the opportunity to meander through the house one last time, taking in each room. I wanted to say goodbye to Lydia, but she was nowhere to be seen. I found Mima in her bedroom getting ready for church.

"We're going to the airport now," I said. I waited for her to look up. After a few minutes, she finally came toward me.

"Be a good girl," she said with a quick pat, then continued dressing.

I had watched her many times with my father before he left for work, so I knew she wasn't into mushy goodbyes. I also knew it had to be torture for her, letting us go and not knowing if she'd ever see us again. And yet, I had hoped for something more. All those years of my childhood, and Mima, still not able to work out how to show that she loved me—it was a knot so tight that it has taken me my whole life to unravel.

"I will, Mima. Goodbye."

I turned and walked out the front door.

Nené had borrowed a car and found a chauffeur for us. Early Monday morning, May 28, 1962, Nené, Mario, and I were driven to the airport. It felt grand, as though we were departing in style. That feeling quickly vanished when we rounded the corner and saw the crowds of people standing in long lines that had formed for food. Ration books had been distributed, and they had already started limiting our family's food, milk, clothing, and household products.

As we neared the airport, I caught sight of the blue and white Pan Am airplane and felt a thrill. I don't know what Mario was feeling, because he sat quietly beside me. The chauffeur dropped us off at the curb. I caught my reflection in the side of the shiny car as it drove away.

We entered the airport terminal, and Nené steered us toward the ticket counter. He checked our suitcase, and we headed toward the gate.

He stopped before we got in line.

"This is as far as I can go."

He knelt down and hugged us both. He held us tightly and wept, which made me cry, too. Then he pressed his forehead to mine as a cat might, kissed us both, and stood.

"I'll see you soon," he said, still wiping his eyes.

We rambled through the line behind a glass wall. Mario and I were led down a long, wide corridor by several airport officials. Just before we rounded the corner, I looked back at Nené one last time. Both of his arms were raised, and he waved wildly. The officials nudged me around the corner. I turned toward the plane and never looked back.

Chapter EIGHT

"You just think lovely wonderful thoughts,"
Peter explained, "and they lift you up in the air."
— J.M. Barrie, *Peter Pan*

Mario and I boarded the plane, and I sat beside him near the window. It was hot and crowded with adults and what looked like ten other Peter Pan children. Some sobbed, others stared straight ahead or into their laps. A little girl who sat directly across the aisle from us moaned and trembled in her seat. The stewardess leaned over her and tried to soothe her, but it was no use.

I wasn't afraid, but rather toe-tapping excited, like the moment before you rip the paper from a Christmas present. Like the promise of sunshine on the other side of fog. I believed what Nené had told me wholeheartedly—everything was going to be fine, and our family would be together again very soon. I had no idea that was not to be the case.

A tall stewardess with dark brown hair and brown eyes leaned over me and Mario. She wore a royal blue Pan Am dress, a blue pill box hat and long white gloves. She was so elegant that for a moment I thought she might have been Jackie Kennedy. She smiled and handed me a cocktail napkin.

"Would you like a coke?" she asked me in Spanish.

"Sí, gracias."

I knew what coke was, but I had never tasted it. She poured me and Mario each a glass of the fizzy brown liquid. As I brought it to my mouth, the bubbles misted my face. It was cold and sweet. I angled toward the window and watched the ground speed by, and then suddenly we were lifted into the air. While the children around me wept, I sat back, marveled at the creaminess of the clouds and savored my drink. I tried to talk to Mario a few times, but he never looked at me or responded. He just stared at the back of the seat in front of him. It was as if we were two separate ships that sailed side by side toward the same new shore.

My stomach fluttered as the wheels touched down. Once we were led off the plane and through customs, I noticed three men who held a sign with our names written on it. One of them, the tallest of the three, pointed to us, waved, and raced over to greet us.

"Mario and Caty, I'm Angel. This is Mauricio and Roger. We're friends of your brother Pete. He asked us to pick you up. Here, let me take your suitcase."

Mario handed Angel the suitcase. All three men were black, muscular and handsome, and all of them wore shorts and light pastel linen *guayaberas*. Those buttoned-up shirts with their intricately embroidered patterns up both front panels are commonly worn by men in Cuba. It was comforting to see them on Pete's friends here in Miami, too.

"Let's go," Angel said.

I rambled wide eyed behind the men through the busy terminal trying to take it all in. Everywhere I turned there were elegantly dressed men and women, new noises, strange languages, profound colors, and strange smells. It was too much to take in all at once, and I stopped walking. The men came back to me.

"Are you feeling all right?" Roger asked.

There were so many things to see: T-shirts and glossy magazines, televisions and food. The food! There was food everywhere. A few hours before, I had seen people in Havana standing in line to scrimp a ration of milk for their babies, and just a few miles away, there was such an abundance of food.

"Yes, I—"

Just then I spotted her—a doll in a store window that was the most beautiful thing I had ever clapped my eyes on. She was as big as I was. Her eyes were powder blue, and her hair was long and silky and golden. Her multicolored dress sparkled like water droplets riding a rainbow. I was spellbound.

Mauricio took my hand. "Come on, Caty. We have to go."

For some reason, it was as if I had suddenly become super charged. I released Mauricio's hand and ran in circles around Mario and the men with my arms outstretched as though I was flying. I was flying. I was free. Like a young balloon out on a holiday. I whooped and cheered, and then all at once, I ground to a halt. Pete's friends stood next to a moving staircase.

"Come on, Caty," Roger said. "There's nothing to be afraid of."

I shook my head. "That thing looks like it would eat people alive."

"No, it's very safe," Angel said. "I'll show you." He stepped onto the escalator, and his body slowly sunk. "See?" he said just before he disappeared.

I moved closer, but noticed the steel-toothed steps that shot out from some unseen opening and backed away. While the rest rode the escalator down, I happily took the stairs.

"I'll go get the car," Angel said.

We stepped outside the terminal and stood on the curb in the sun to wait for Angel. Sharp, thirsty grass forced its way up through the concrete here and there, like a quiet invasion. The air was sticky and heavy-hot, almost fuzzy, as though it quivered. With all that humidity, my pretty flat hair erupted into wild steel wool, and there was nothing I could do about it.

Angel pulled up in a dark blue car, and I climbed into back seat.

"Where are we going?" I asked.

"To a camp for children," Angel said. "It's not far from here."

He pulled onto the highway, and I rolled down the window. The sun-blasted shrubs along the side of the road were dotted with yellow flowers. Soon afterward, we pulled onto a dirt road and drove through a chain link fence. A large Cuban flag sighed from a steel flagpole just inside the entrance. The camp was a cluster of two-story, flat-roofed cement buildings. On either side of each was a wooden staircase that led to the second floor. A long walkway ran the length of the fronts of the buildings. They looked like small motels. Angel parked, and we got out of the car.

A few other cars had arrived carrying other Peter Pan kids from our flight. Angel motioned for us all to gather together.

"Good morning, kids," he spoke to us in Spanish. "This is the Catholic Welfare Bureau camp in Florida City or the CWB. Each building holds about twenty children. The boys' dorm rooms are on one side, the girls' dorms were on the other. Everyone is assigned an adult couple who will watch over you. You are all assigned to Mr. and Mrs. Sanchez. Here they are now."

A middle-aged man and woman approached us. Mr. Sanchez was stocky with a face the color of cheese. He wore his pants so high that his belt rested just below his breast bone. His dark hair was greased and combed straight back. He wore thick black framed glasses and a gold pinky ring on his right hand. Mrs. Sanchez was thin and had olive skin and a helmet of curls the color of wood soaked by the rain. She wore blue cat eye glasses and a blue and white striped sleeveless dress.

"Follow me, boys," Mr. Sanchez said in Spanish. "The girls will go with Mrs. Sanchez."

"Come, girls," she called over her shoulder. She waved her hand for us to follow her as though she was swatting impatiently at flies. We trailed her up the flight of stairs and down the walkway then into a large dorm room with bunk beds stacked one on top of another.

"Please drop off your things, and come right back downstairs. You can play outside until lunch is ready. Caty, since you're the smallest, I want you to take one of the lower bunks."

Mario had taken our suitcase, so I had nothing to drop off. I chose a nearby bunk and followed her downstairs. I plunked down on the steps and watched a group of girls play in the grass near the fence. One of them, a chubby girl with salted caramel skin and straight black hair, glanced over at me. She appeared to be a few years older than me. She whispered something into the huddle of girls. Their giggles bubbled up, then like a herd of deer, they all snapped their heads my way. They sauntered over and mobilized at the bottom of the stairs.

"What's your name?" the chubby girl asked.

"Bienvenida Catalina Miranda. What's yours?"

"Vivian Ruiloba." Her nose crinkled as she looked me up and down. "So, what are you, a Santería?"

"No. I'm Catholic."

"What's with the white dress?"

"It's blue and white—the colors of the Virgin."

"The Virgin! That's rich. Hey, girls, get a load of the Virgin." She looked back at me with a smirk. "Well, *Bienvenida*, welcome."

Vivian and the girls snickered as they walked away, and I felt a sudden sting. A nicked finger in a pickle jar. A sister wearing an all-white habit marched out into the yard.

"Lunch is ready," she hollered and went inside.

I followed the girls into the cafeteria and sat down at the end of a long wooden table. Several adults swooped between us and doled out ham sandwiches and milk. Even though I was away from home, there were so many Cubans at the camp who spoke Spanish in a Cuban accent, it was as though we were simply in a different neighborhood of Havana.

That night, I changed into my pajamas and laid down in my bunk. As soon as the lights flickered off, I heard a girl start to cry somewhere in the dark. Then two girls. Then three. Soon the room throbbed with the sounds of sobbing and calls for "Mami." I was overwhelmed with a sadness that seemed to seep from my bones—not only for the loss of home and family, but for something more, something I couldn't pinpoint. I buried my face into the pillow and cried myself to sleep.

There are certain unseen events that happen in life that instantly propel you down a different path. A few nights later, I experienced one of those events. I was the youngest girl in our dorm room, but also the only black girl. Most were teenagers, and you know how teenage girls are. If they aren't with boys, they are either dreaming about boys or talking about them. As soon as the lights were turned off, the older girls started the yickity yacking.

"Will you please shut up," someone said. "We're trying to get some sleep."

For reasons known only to God, I added, "Yeah, and if you don't shut up, I'm going to throw a shoe at you."

Well, they didn't shut up. And I threw the shoe. It hit one of the girls in the side of the head. One of them must have left the room and told Mr. Sanchez, because before long, he blasted through the door and slapped on the lights.

"I want all of you girls to sit down and listen to me carefully. I don't want any monkey business while you are here. When the lights go off, I want every one of you in your beds fast asleep. Am I making myself perfectly clear?"

No one said a word. We sat on our beds and blinked at him like owls.

"Caty, walk with me."

I followed him out the door onto the walkway. As soon the door shut behind him, he spun around, and his eyes flashed at me like two hot coins. He knelt down beside me. His breath smelled like stale smoke. He grabbed me by the arm and dug his fingers into the tender underside.

"Listen to me," he said. "Be very careful, Caty. This isn't Cuba. Things are different for you here and not in good way. The rules are different for you because you are black. You will be sorely mistreated if you misbehave in such a fashion. Here, you have to obey the whites and do whatever they tell you to do, mind your own business, and keep your mouth shut." He clamped both hands on my shoulders and shook hard. "Do you understand me?"

I was stunned and felt my eyes prick with tears. "No."

"Well, you don't have to understand. You just have to play by the rules."

I knew I shouldn't have thrown the shoe, but I had no idea what he was talking about. Rules? What rules? Who made up these rules? How was I supposed to follow them if I had no idea what they were?

Mr. Sanchez stood and steered me back into the room. I sat down on my bed and watched him barrel toward the door. Just before he left, he turned and glared at me over the top of his glasses and then smacked off the lights.

That Sunday, the adults arranged for all of us to have an outing at the beach. It was warm, and the wind pulled feathery clouds across the dark blue sky. One of the men stood in front of us and blew a whistle.

"Okay, listen up," he said. "Whoever wants to go swimming, please stand in this line. Those who don't want to swim, stand over there in that line."

Imagine, I had lived on an island my whole life, but I had never been in the water. I never even owned a bathing suit, but I shot over and stood in the swimming line. They led us out to the ocean, and I stood at the shore and stared at the glossy-grey water. I felt the cool cream of the surf wash over my feet. The surge sucked the sand back out through my toes. I bent over and brushed my hands across the lapping water and brought my fingers up to my mouth and tasted the salt. I stood and focused my gaze over the swimmers and beyond, out to where the sky met the sea. Sunlight reflected off the wave tips like a string of diamonds. I didn't try to swim that day. I only got my feet wet, but I could have died and gone straight to heaven.

That afternoon as we drove back to the camp, I daydreamed about the following Sunday. I couldn't wait to go back to the beach. But it wasn't to be. Little did I know, in four days I would be living somewhere else.

Chapter NINE

"Wake up, Caty." Mrs. Sanchez whispered as she shook my shoulder. "Gather your things, and meet me downstairs."

I tumbled into my dress and stepped out onto the walkway. The smooth face of the moon nodded toward the dark horizon. The sun had not yet risen, and it was chilly and damp. Several boys and girls clumped at the bottom of the stairs. Mario was there, too, rubbing sleep from his eyes. All the children gathered were black. There were no white children anywhere to be seen.

Mrs. Sanchez led us to the dining room. As we ate breakfast, several adults stood with their backs against the wall, glancing at their watches. As soon as we were finished, they led us outside, and Mrs. Sanchez gestured toward several vans.

"Boys in those van, girls in these."

I followed four other girls into one of the vans, but before I climbed in, I turned back to Mrs. Sanchez.

"Where are we going?" I asked.

She must not have heard me, because she shooed me in and swung the doors shut without looking at me. Frances Cuevas sat beside me in the way back. She was eight years old and plump with soft, curly hair. Her sister Maria sat in the middle seat in front of us. She was twelve and slender with long, kinky hair and skin the color of crème brûlée barely toasted. Beside her sat a tiny eight-year-old girl named Juana Blanco who started to cry. Maria put her arm around Juana to settle her. The fifth girl was Vivian Ruiloba. I later found out she was eleven years old. From the day I arrived, Vivian seemed to take pleasure in pricking my peace, but not that day.

The driver adjusted his rearview mirror then threw an elbow over the back of the seat to get a good look at us.

"Everybody in?" he asked over his sunglasses. Before we could respond, he spun back around, thumped the gas pedal and turned the key. He peeled through the opening in the chain link fence. I looked back at the camp and watched it disappear in a cloud of dust. We bumped through scrubland for what seemed like a month. We finally pulled onto the highway, and I spotted the airport.

"Are we going home?" I asked.

"Not yet. You're going to a different home for a little while."

He veered into the airport and parked the car along the curb outside a terminal. A jumble of adults swooped toward the van and herded us into the airport. Tickets were thrust into our hands, and we boarded a Delta Airlines plane. I found a seat next to the window and scanned heads to find Mario. He was seated with the boys several rows behind me. He spotted me and nodded. I nodded back and settled into my seat. An hour later, we touched down in New Orleans. It was Thursday, June 7th, and we had been in the United States ten days.

We were led to the arrivals gate where another huddle of adults had shuffled together a large group of black and white children. A few men and women worked their way through the group separating whites from blacks and boys from girls. The white children were led away by white adults. Several black men hustled Mario and the rest of the black boys toward the parking lot. I tried to get Mario's attention, but three black sisters suddenly materialized in front of me. Beside them was a white priest and a tall, white man in regular street clothes. The tall man stepped forward.

"Good morning, ladies," he said in Spanish. "Please, don't be frightened. I am Mr. Ramos." I could tell by his accent that he was Cuban. "This is Father Michael Coffey, Sister Fabian, Sister Paulette and our Mother Superior, Mother Clement Marie. We're going to take you girls home."

Father Coffey bent forward at his waist and shook my hand. He was a broad man with soft shiny black hair, like a cat's, and eyes the color of the sea after a storm. While he shook the other girls' hands, I stared at the sisters. I had never seen black sisters before. They all wore black tunics belted at the waist, white scapulars that draped their shoulders and white wimples that circled their faces. Many years later, I saw the same habit on Whoopi Goldberg in the movie *Sister Act.*

Sister Fabian shook our hands and nodded at each one of us. She was a short, round woman with kind eyes. As she leaned toward Father to whisper in his ear, I noticed a Dowager's Hump above her shoulder blades. She said something that I didn't understand in a low, husky voice.

Sister Paulette was the next to shake our hands. She was very thin and delicate with caramel skin and beautiful Asian eyes.

Finally, Mother Clement Marie hobbled forward on two metal crutches that clamped her forearms. I found out later she suffered from debilitating arthritis. The tiny curls at her temple that had escaped her wimple were the color of smoke and ash. When she smiled, her dark cheeks puffed liked risen bread reducing her eyes to two chicks. She looked like a black Mother Teresa.

"Come with us," Mr. Ramos said.

We followed them to the parking lot where the sun bore down on the cars like a curse. I slipped into the back seat of Father's dark green car, and the vinyl scorched my legs. Hot wind whipped through the open windows as we sailed down the highway. Mr. Ramos lit a cigarette, and each time he exhaled, a feather of smoke swirled out his open window back into mine. He swiveled toward us every now and then and smiled.

"Is my family here?" I asked.

"No. You're going to live at a girls' orphanage for a while."

"But I'm not an orphan."

"It's not that kind of an orphanage. It's a beautiful place with girls of all different ages who will make you feel right at home."

"Where is my brother, Mario?"

"He'll be staying just down the road at the Lafon Home for Boys."

We swung off the highway and slowed in front of a huge three-story red brick house at 2710 Gentilly Boulevard. An apron of green grass circled the house, and small hedges trimmed into neat circles edged the front sidewalk. To the left of the wooden banister that led to the front porch, a large blue and white statue of the Virgin Mary stood in the front yard with her arms outstretched in welcome.

Father pulled into the driveway along the back of the house. Scrawny shrubs attempted a prison break underneath a chain link fence that surrounded the large back yard. There were swing sets, toys, and bicycles everywhere.

"Here we are," Mr. Ramos said. "This way."

We followed Mr. Ramos and Sister Paulette through a door underneath a grand set of cement stairs that led up to the outdoor patio on the second floor. As soon as we entered, a few girls stopped whatever they were doing and stared at us. In Cuba, people's skin colors ranged from very white to very dark and everything in between. These girls' skin colors were different shades, too, but they were all considered black.

"This is the St. John Berchmans Orphanage for Girls, and it's run by the Sisters of the Holy Family who have dedicated their lives to care for black people. On the first floor under these stairs is the pantry," Mr. Ramos said. "On the right is the sisters' dining room, and on the left, is the dining room for you girls."

In the girls' dining room, I saw twelve light wooden tables that had been buffed with wax and hunkered on white tiled floors that shone like mirrors. The pine cleaner that sweetened the air reminded me of the time we drove through lush evergreen forests on our way to visit family in Pinar del Río.

"Off to the side of the sisters' dining room is the kitchen."

I could see two sisters in the kitchen preparing food. Just then, my hunger flared. We had been served a snack on the plane, but seeing that food made me ravenous. There was a huge walk-in refrigerator in the kitchen. I could see that beyond the kitchen, there were two large open rooms.

"There are about sixty girls living here ranging from small babies to late teens. Ten sisters live here with you girls. Each sister is assigned a certain age group. Sister Paulette, here, is your den mother. Father Coffey lives here, too."

As Mr. Ramos continued his tour speaking to us over his shoulder, a little black dog ran past us down the hall. Its nails clickity clacked across the tiles.

"That's Blackie. He's very friendly. He belongs to one of the girls here named Martha Cadre whose Aunt Rose is the cook."

We followed Mr. Ramos and Sister Paulette through a toy-littered playroom with floor tiles that were black with colored speckles. We continued through to a sewing room with several racks of clothes like you'd see in a department store. Sister Fabian had made her way to the sewing room and bellied up to a table piled high with clothes. She smiled at us and warble-whistled as she stabbed a sock with a needle. I couldn't whistle. I tried once, but Mima smacked me hard and reprimanded me for trying. She said it was unladylike and that only boys should be allowed to whistle.

"Beside the laundry room is the bathroom and showers," Mr. Ramos said. "You will each have a cabinet beside your bed for your personal items, but the clothes on this rack are for everyone to share. We don't believe in vanity or being wasteful here. Whenever anyone outgrows their own clothes, they are mended and placed on this rack for others to use. This way, you always have clothing regardless of whether you own it or borrow it. If you want to wear something from this rack, feel free to wear whatever fits you."

We followed him and Sister Paulette up a flight of stairs.

"Here we have the second floor which is the main floor," he said.

We gathered just inside the front door at the bottom of a large wooden staircase that swooped up into the belly of the house. The rooms on either side of the staircase were open and airy with walls painted in creamy tones, colorful artwork, and lush potted plants. Sunlight moted through the window glass. To me, it looked like a palace.

"On this floor, you'll find an auditorium, Father Coffey's apartment, the sisters' parlor, the library, and the main parlor for guests."

Two girls burst through the front door and whooshed past us and up the stairs. The house echoed with laughter and the sound of shoes clapping against wooden floors and music and chatter. The house pulsed with sweet energy. Words flowed like water over stone. I had heard a few English expressions in Cuba, but never an entire conversation.

We followed Mr. Ramos and Sister Paulette up the staircase to the third floor. The old wood sang a tired symphony of creaks and moans. We draggled behind Mr. Ramos down the hall and into a small chapel. It was dark with plum-colored walls and warm wooden pews that angled away from the miniature altar like an arrow. The crucifixion in stained glass glowed behind the tabernacle in back of the altar.

"Mass is held here first thing every morning," Mr. Ramos said. We followed him into the hall, and he gestured to the right.

"The sisters' dorm is that way along with the nursery and Mother Clement Marie's office."

He turned to the left and motioned for us to follow. He pointed toward a room in the middle of the floor.

"This is the infirmary. You'll sleep here tonight."

"But I'm not sick," Vivian said.

"I know. It's only for one night while they prepare your beds. Come along." He led us to the end of a long hall. "These three rooms are the girls' dorms. The blue one is for the girls your age, the green one is for the smaller girls, and the yellow one is for the older girls."

We entered the blue room. There were about fifteen beds, and on each of the beds was a blue bedspread. Tucked in front of each pillow was a caramel-colored teddy bear. Beside the beds were small wooden cabinets, and on the wall above each bed was a small shelf.

"There's a bathroom on each floor for you to share."

We followed him through a door in the hallways that led to an outdoor porch that stretched the entire length of the back of the building. Plants hugged a fancy whitewashed wrought iron railing.

"There's a porch just like this below us on the second floor."

We followed Mr. Ramos and Sister Paulette down the stairs and huddled together by the front door.

"That's it for the tour. I have to go now, but I'll be back soon to check up on you."

As soon as the door closed behind Mr. Ramos, Sister Paulette's smile vanished. She said something to us in English that none of us understood and pushed us toward the stairs that led to the first floor. She herded us back toward the laundry room and motioned toward the showers. We stood there frozen, staring at her. Sister hooked Vivian's elbow and led her to the shower, motioned for her to undress, then pointed for her to get in.

I've never been one to be shy about bathroom activities. After all, I grew up in a crowded apartment where my family all used a chamber pot. Still, I was embarrassed to strip in front of perfect strangers. Maria helped me unfasten the back buttons. As soon as my lovely new dress slipped to the floor, Sister Paulette snatched it, crumpled it into a ball, and walked away. I stepped into the shower and washed off quickly.

After we shuffled out of the shower, Sister Paulette handed us towels and pointed to the neat stacks of clothes for us to wear. In my stack there was fresh underwear, yellow shorts, a white blouse and pink plastic Flip Flops. I had never worn anything other than a dress and socks and shoes, but I didn't dare say a word.

After we dressed, Sister motioned for us to sit down at the mending table. She paced in front of us, inspecting. When her eyes landed on me, she scowled. She may have appeared small and delicate, but there was nothing dainty about her. She scraped a chair up beside me and grabbed a comb with tough plastic teeth and raked it across my head.

"Ouch!"

She snapped my shoulder hard with the comb. I was so shocked, but I never made another sound. Tears stung my eyes as she ripped and tugged my hair into a tight braid.

After we had been scrubbed, dressed and pawed within an inch of our lives, we were led outside to the back yard, presumably to play with the other girls, though none of us felt much like playing. My head throbbed from the yanking.

We sat together in the grass off to the side. I watched an ant carry a butterfly wing in its pinchers through the grass like a flag. A grey squirrel zigzagged across the yard and then paused on his hind legs to contemplate his next move. The wind kicked up, and the trees tossed their heads and jostled their limbs. A few flower petals along the back fence unlatched.

At 5:00 p.m., a tall, wiry sister appeared beside the back door. She lifted a large, brass bell, hammered it once then disappeared back inside. The girls abandoned whatever they were doing and ran toward the house. We followed them inside and down the hall into the bathroom to wash our hands, then to the dining hall. We Cuban girls sat together. I tried to focus on facial expressions in order to guess what everyone was saying. I was terrified, exhausted, and starving.

A cart rolled between the tables with sliced breads, peanut butter and jelly, luncheon meats, tomato slices, condiments, and small cartons of milk. We watched the girls take a carton of milk and whatever they wanted to make themselves sandwiches.

While we ate, a broad, stocky sister drifted between each of the tables like an iceberg. She held a large wooden paddle in her right hand and smacked it against her left palm. She glared at the girls as though at any moment if someone got out of line, she'd give them a good hard whack. She wafted in our direction, and her eyes found mine and flashed two warnings. My stomach went oily. As she approached our table, I lowered my eyes onto my plate. I didn't think I was doing anything wrong, but I certainly didn't want to find out the hard way.

After dinner, Sister Paulette motioned for us to follow her up the stairs. She led us to the infirmary and pointed toward the beds. On each bed was a folded blanket and a nightgown. We each picked a bed and sat down. I had a sudden image of Mima back home in her bedroom listening to the news on her radio, and Nené reading the newspaper in the living room, and Lydia asleep in our bed by herself, and Pete, who I hoped was safe and still in hiding.

Sister glared down her nose at us, her pupils two moons of black. Tears puddled my eyes before I could stop them. With my glazed vision, I watched Sister's image turn softer and softer as she marched toward the door. She flicked out the light and was gone.

Chapter TEN

The next morning at 5:30 a.m., Sister Paulette burst through the infirmary door, clapped her hands and snatched the blankets off each of our bodies. I hauled my eyelids up for a split second then flopped back onto the pillow and eased the blanket back over my body. Sister had other plans. She jerked the blanket completely off the bed, snapped her fingers at me and pointed toward the door.

I followed the rest of the girls downstairs to the bathroom and washed up while Sister Paulette picked out clothes for us from the rack. She handed me a pair of navy blue shorts, a red top and blue sneakers. I was grateful I wasn't given Flip Flops again, because two angry blisters sulked on the inside of my big toes.

We were led back upstairs to the chapel for daily Mass. We filed into the pews, took our seats, and waited for mass to begin. One of the sisters, whose name I found out later was Sister Helena, sat at the organ. She was skinny and had a gap-toothed smile. As Father entered the chapel, the organ yawned a hymn, and we all stood. Going to church as often as I did, I knew the structure of the Mass in my sleep, but I had no idea what Father and the girls were saying. My tongue flipped and rolled in unfamiliar ways. I tasted the new words and let them flow from my mouth and join the others in a swirl that rose like incense.

After mass, we paraded downstairs to the dining room and took our seats. I could see down the hallway into the kitchen where several sisters swooped in circles from the stove to platters resting on the counter top. A chubby woman, who I assumed was Aunt Rose, gave orders with the flip of her spatula. The sisters then carried out steaming piles of pancakes droopy with butter and syrup while a few more sisters followed with pitchers of cold milk.

Once our plates were cleaned, we were pointed out back to the yard to play. Until we became familiar enough to belong to the orphanage, the girls eyed us with a degree of uncertainty, so we Cuban girls sat off to the side again and watched. At noon, another sister appeared with the brass bell to ring in lunchtime. This time, instead of sitting down at the table, the girls stood silently behind their chairs. I scanned the room, waiting for something to happen. Mother Clement Marie began to recite what I later found out was called the Angelus Prayer:

Sister: The Angel of the Lord declared to Mary
Girls: And she conceived of the Holy Spirit.
Everyone: Hail Mary, full of grace, the Lord is with thee; blessed art thou among women and blessed is the fruit of thy womb, Jesus. Holy Mary, Mother of God, pray for us sinners, now and at the hour of our death. Amen.
Sister: Behold the handmaid of the Lord: Be it done unto me according to Thy word.
Everyone: Hail Mary, full of grace, the Lord is with thee; blessed art thou among women and blessed is the fruit of thy womb, Jesus. Holy Mary, Mother of God, pray for us sinners, now and at the hour of our death. Amen.
Sister: And the Word was made Flesh: And dwelt among us.
Everyone: Hail Mary, full of grace, the Lord is with thee; blessed art thou among women and blessed is the fruit of thy womb, Jesus. Holy Mary, Mother of God, pray for us sinners, now and at the hour of our death. Amen.
Sister: Pray for us, O Holy Mother of God, that we may be made worthy of the promises of Christ. Let us pray. Pour forth, we beseech Thee, O Lord, thy grace into our hearts; that we, to whom the incarnation of Christ, Thy Son, was made known by the message of an angel, may by His Passion and Cross be brought to the glory of His Resurrection, through the same Christ Our Lord.
Everyone: Amen.

After lunch, the sisters got busy training us new girls up. Mother Clement Marie pulled me aside and motioned for me to follow her upstairs. She reached into a utility closet and handed me a broom and a watering can. I followed her out onto the third-floor patio. She pointed to the broom then to the floor, and I nodded. Then she took the watering can and sprinkled water over the plants. I nodded again. She then pointed to her watch, which I understood meant that she wanted me to do this chore every day at the same time, so I nodded again. Then she waved me off.

The house buzzed with the noise of all those girls. The sounds in our house back home were more subdued—brooms skimming tiled floors, knives chopping vegetables, sheets snapping high in the air before they billowed down onto mattresses. I missed the rhythmic music that shimmied from Mima's radio. The orphanage smelled different, too. Whereas fresh soap and rich fried foods perfumed our house, the orphanage smelled like pine cleaner and Aunt Rose's baking—which wasn't unpleasant. Just new and strange.

That evening, we Cuban girls were shown our beds in the blue dorm. Mine was in the middle of the row on the outside wall right underneath the window. A sister was stationed in the bedroom to watch over us in the night. Our guardian was Sister Angela, a skinny woman with bright eyes and a quick smile. Her bed and nightstand were situated in a corner of the room by the door behind a wall divider. She sat in the doorway between the blue and green rooms and waited for everyone to wash up, get in their PJs, and climb into bed. Once everyone was settled for the night, she turned off the lights.

The night was jungle-hot, and the cicadas shrieked from the black tree tops. I laid on my belly, my body hum-tired, and I looked up at the bright yellow moon. It had risen just above the trees and hung lazy in the night sky as though it floated on a string. I longed for my family and wondered if they were looking at the same moon, too. I was far from everything I knew, far from myself.

I suddenly noticed that the girl in the bed next to mine was smiling at me. She wore a white nightgown with blue ribbons at the neck. She looked like a doll with light, delicate features and straight black hair. She said something in English to me that I didn't understand, so I shrugged.

"Martha Cadre," she said, placing her hand on her chest.

"Blackie."

"Yes."

"Catalina," I said with my hand on my chest.

Her eyebrows scrunched.

"Caty."

She nodded. "Good night, Caty."

She fluffed her pillow and tucked the cotton sheet under her chin.

"Good night, Martha."

I rolled onto my back and smiled. That was my first English sentence.

Sister Angela's alarm clock roared at 5:30 a.m. I groaned and pulled the blanket over my head. After trying that move with Sister Paulette, I should have known that behavior wasn't going to fly. Sister ripped the blanket from my bed and thrust clothes into my arms. I quickly dressed and followed the girls out of the room.

After mass, we scuffled downstairs to the dining room for breakfast. I soon found out just how resourceful the sisters were. They made deals with the local merchants to pick up day-old food that was next to nothing or for free. That morning, they had gone to the bakery and brought back day-old donuts, and Aunt Rose refreshed them in the oven. The sisters doled out cold milk and hot donuts like bread and wine. It cost them nothing and yet it meant so much to us. I've always thought that the sisters and the priests are mystics among us going about the sacred muddle of the everyday without any fuss.

After breakfast, we were all expected to do our chores. It might sound strange, but I looked forward to doing my chores, because I wanted to belong. The sisters ran a tight ship, and it was a well-oiled machine. Their discipline reminded me of Mima and how she ran our house back home. It made me feel comfortable. I knew my place. I knew what was expected of me. I knew I fit in.

Unfortunately, I didn't always understand my instructions. While playing cards with Frances Cuevas one afternoon in the playroom, Sister Paulette grabbed me by the arm and dragged me to the third-floor patio. She pointed to the plants that I had been watering every day for two weeks. They were all dead. She shook her head at the plants and again at me.

"No plants," she said. She pushed a broom in my hands and pointed to the stairs.

I nodded, and she walked away muttering.

I soon figured out that she wanted me to sweep the stairs every day and wash them on Saturdays. I had stair duty until the end of the month, then we all switched chores. The following month, I was given kitchen duty, which meant that every day I washed the dishes after every meal. While one girl was responsible for the floors, another did the ironing, and another did the sewing, and then we'd switch again. The house thrummed with the business of chores: the swish of hands in mop water, the clink of clean dishes restacked in the cupboards, the soft white noise of the vacuum cleaner, the tap-tap-tap of the sewing machine needle into worn clothes. No one grumbled. That just wasn't allowed. There simply was no time for it. The sisters wanted each of us to know how to successfully run a house, but it wasn't just that. They taught us how to care for ourselves and our future homes with both discipline and pride. Those sisters were tough but brilliant.

After our chores were finished, we were shooed out into the back yard. I began to play with the other girls—on the swing set, or in games like hide-n-seek, jacks, and Old Maid—and somehow, I was able to communicate. Nobody helped us Cuban girls with English, but we took to it like bees to honey and within no time, we were speaking English well.

Father taught all of us how to ride a bike. Like everything else, we were thrown in the deep end. We were each placed on the seat, told to pedal hard and were pushed forward. We crashed of course, but we learned to ride quickly without training wheels.

One morning, I spotted Martha Cadre off to the side of the yard, so I sat beside her in the grass. An older girl joined us.

"This is Paulette," Martha said motioning toward the girl. "She's my sister. She's fifteen."

Like Martha, Paulette had light skin and beautiful straight black hair. I found out later that the Cadres were mulattos, which by the way, is not a derogatory term. It simply means that the person has both European and African ancestry. Mulatto does not derive from the word "mule" which I have heard some people say. That would be translated as mulas, not mulattos. The word mulatto actually comes from the Arabic "muwallad," which means "a person of mixed ancestry."[23] This is probably what the majority of us will eventually look like generations from now by mixing all our races together. And I think that's fabulous.

"Nice to meet you," Paulette said. She stared at my head.

"What is it?" I asked.

She pointed. "What's going on with your hair?"

"I know. It's terrible. My mother used to iron it flat and put it into braids for me, but I don't know how."

Paulette took my hand and led me to a small brick building in the corner of the back yard. Inside there were pink reclining chairs beneath sinks along the back wall, black swivel chairs in front of large mirrors and a row of yellow upholstered chairs with hooded dryers against another wall. We both spotted a glittery pink barrette on the floor beside one of the swivel chairs. She scooped it up and stashed it in her pocket.

"This is our beauty salon," Paulette said. "Girls from the beauty school come after their classes and work on our hair for free."

A tall black woman stood behind a swivel chair trimming one of the girl's hair. Paulette motioned for me to sit in a free swivel chair. She picked up a comb and gently worked it through my hair, then began to braid. After she was finished, she handed me a mirror and spun the chair around so I could see the back.

"What do you think?"

"They're the prettiest braids I've ever seen." I handed her back the mirror. "Why are you helping me?"

"Because you're letting me."

The following morning, and every morning afterward, Paulette came to our bedroom first thing and did my hair for me.

For many, the word "orphanage" is a bleak word. It implies loss, abandonment, guilt, and shame. It's devastating for a child to lose their parents, but then to not have any loving family members able to take them in after such a loss is a blow from which some never recover. And at that time, when an unwed girl found herself "in trouble," families often shamed them into giving their babies away to orphanages. It was also common for families who fell on hard times to place their children in orphanages if they no longer could afford them. I found out that that was the case for Martha Cadre and her siblings Anna, Maria, Paulette, Lois, and Cecilia who lived at our orphanage. Their brother Oliver was sent to live in the Lafon Home for Boys where Mario stayed. They had a baby sister who stayed behind at home with their mother. I couldn't image the thought of my family living in the same city and never being reunited with them.

I remember the first time I heard a baby being dropped off at the orphanage. It was in the middle of the night and for some reason I couldn't sleep. There was a knock on the front door. I heard one of the sisters get up and go downstairs. I got out of bed and tiptoed past Sister Angela who was snoring. I stood in the open door and leaned my ear into the hall. I heard muffled voices float up the stairs—the sister's and another woman's voice. The woman's voice shook, and she began to cry.

"Go back to bed, Catalina," Sister Angela said.

"What's happening?"

Sister Angela sat up. "I imagine another poor girl has gotten herself into trouble."

"Is she all right?"

"That's none of your affair. Now go back to bed."

The sisters took in the black babies and tried to find them good homes. As it turned out, all of our babies at our orphanage had families. Either they came from unwed mothers, or like the Cadres, both parents were alive and well and living right there in New Orleans. Those dear babies weren't orphans but orphaned. Many times, the mothers who cowered at our nighttime door wanted desperately to keep their babies, but their families forbade them to do so. I overheard one of the sisters once tell one of the toddlers that her mother had given her up because she loved her too much. It wasn't the case, of course. They simply couldn't care for them as well as an intact nuclear family could.

The problem with telling those children that lie is that many of those babies then equated love with abandonment. And because most, if not all, of the adoptions at that time were closed adoptions, the stigma and pain of that secrecy never left them. Although those babies might grow up to become happy, productive adults, that niggle, that shadow of the past trauma never quite leaves them, as though it had wriggled down under the skin into their very DNA.

Although my family sent me and Mario away, it was different for us than for the Cadres and those poor little babies. To me, the orphanage felt like a mansion. And I sensed in my bones that my family would one day be together again. It was that hope that kept me going.

A few months had passed, and I was finally allowed to visit Mario for the first time with Paulette as my chaperone. It was a warm Saturday morning, and we walked one block to St. Anthony Avenue and waited at the bus stop. As we sat on the bench together, Paulette stood and walked over by the grass. Something had caught her eye. She leaned over to pick it up then sat back down next to me. She showed me a shiny gold button.

"Why did you pick that up?"

She shrugged, examined the button in her palm for a second, then dropped it in her pocket. I later found out that Paulette collected all kinds of shiny worthless things that she found and kept them in a drawer beside her bed.

The city bus pulled up, and I followed Paulette onto the bus. I watched as she dropped coins into the glass box next to the driver. He handed her two tickets, and I flopped into the front seat and settled in next to the window.

I suddenly felt a sharp pain. Paulette stood in the aisle, eyes gaping, and yanked hard on my arm. She jerked her head toward the back of the bus. I shook my head and motioned for her to sit beside me. Instead, she leaned back and pulled my arm so violently that my body slid across the seat, and I was on my feet.

It occurred to me just then that Paulette might actually be mentally unstable. After all, I hadn't known her that long, so who was to say? Then I noticed the other passengers, with furrowed brows and pursed lips flicking their eyes toward the back of the bus. The bus driver eyed us in the rearview mirror and gave an interrogating thumb jerk toward the back of the bus. I glanced back there and realized that all those passengers in the back were black, and that all those in the front were white folks. Paulette and I slipped into a seat in the back. The black folks around us nodded their heads in approval.

In less than ten minutes, we arrived at the boys' orphanage at 6900 Chef Menteur Highway. We were escorted straight to the back yard by a tall black man with rounded shoulders. We sat on the edge of the lawn and watched the boys play kick ball. Mario finally scuffled out from the house and sat down beside me. He looked tired.

"Mario, this is Paulette," I said in English.

"Nice to meet you," he responded in English.

"You, too," she said. She stood and brushed the grass from her skirt and strolled over by the back fence. Mario stared at the grass.

"How are you?" I reverted to Spanish.

"Fine."

"You don't seem fine."

He took a deep breath and sighed. "I feel angry all the time, and I don't know what to do about it. The American boys here are arrogant and treat the Cubans like trash. We hate each other. At least once a day a fight breaks out."

He picked at the grass. "In Cuba, we were taught to be confidence. Here, even though we're all black, there's a pecking order, and we Cubans are on the bottom rung."

"Can you say something to someone?"

He laughed. "No." He stared at a point in the distance. "Oscar and Pablo ran away. They were brothers who came over with us."

His eyes settled back onto the grass. "All we hear from the American boys is 'nigger this and nigger that', and 'who do these niggers think they are?' We're all black! But apparently, you have to be the right shade of black, and according to these people, the lighter the better. Oscar and Pablo are even darker than I am, so I'm not surprised they took off. Truth is, if I had known they were leaving, I might have gone, too."

He popped the head off of a dandelion with his thumb. "I was worried for them. I heard that New Orleans is surrounded by marshes, and that's where they were found—deep in the marshes. I heard they took them somewhere else to live, but I don't know where. Maybe their parents were able to leave Cuba and they're with them."

I looked at Mario and he shrugged. We both knew that wasn't the case.

"Well, that's what I hope anyway."

Mario gazed upward toward the sky, trying to will the tears from overflowing. Seeing him so upset frightened me. At that moment, I longed for a piece of home. I needed to feel how I felt whenever Pipo was home on leave—that no matter what, everything was going to be just fine. I ached for him.

I had to look away and spotted Paulette talking to a boy by the fence. The round-shouldered man shuffled over to her and whispered something to her. She nodded and came over to join us.

"We have to go," she said.

"Okay."

Mario and I stood. We didn't hug because that just wasn't our style, but I knew that we both wanted to.

"See you soon," I said.

Paulette and I made our way back to the bus stop. We boarded the bus, and headed straight for the back. I thought about what Mario said, and I understood his despair. He was insulted and abused simply because his skin was darker than the rest. I *had* to take a seat in the back of the bus, directed there wordlessly by the whites in the front. The blacks all around us sat obediently, their faces as expressionless as water.

Was the back of the bus any better or worse than the front? I didn't think so, but that wasn't the point. Someone else was determining what I could and couldn't do based solely on the color of my skin. My anger was like a hot wire. Tear-blurry houses rushed passed the window. I understood that the world was divided into those who could and those who couldn't. Under the bludgeonings of chance, we blacks got the short straw. I had boarded a bus there'd be no getting off.

Chapter ELEVEN

That summer, I learned about the birds and the bees. Mother Clement Marie hired an OBGYN nurse to come to the orphanage every year. She taught us about our bodies and explained why we had periods. I hadn't gotten mine at that time, but I had known all about it from Lydia. Imagine, in a house full of girls, everyone talked about it. Still, looking back, I think Mother was smart to make sure we all knew the facts. She was quite progressive and ahead of her time for keeping things real with us girls. She was full of love and understanding, so when it finally happened for me, I wasn't afraid in the least.

When I was in Cuba, I remember that there was a custom for women to not wash their hair while they were having their periods. I'm not entirely sure why. I don't think it had anything to do with personal hygiene, but more of a superstition. I have heard that some women thought they'd be too attractive to a man if they washed their hair, so they didn't while they were on their periods. Which is absurd. Men don't care about a woman's hair, if they notice it at all. Truth is, women need a reason to have sex—men just need a place.

During the summer, Father Coffey sometimes took us to the beach on the weekends. He was so much fun to be with. He had a laugh that shook his whole body. There was a lightness to his being, and I knew that whenever we went somewhere with him, we'd have a ball.

"We're going to take you girls on a special excursion today," he announced at breakfast one sunny Wednesday morning.

Our arms flew in the air, and we cheered.

"Are we going to the beach?" one asked.

"No. You're going to spend the day at the white orphanage."

Our arms slowly lowered, and our smiles faded.

"Why?" I asked.

"You girls will have a marvelous time. You'll see."

It was understood that the white children went to all-white orphanages and the black children went to all-black orphanages. There was no mixing. No exceptions. Nevertheless, we piled into the orphanage's beige station wagon complete with the orphanage's logo painted on both sides. Father drove us across town to the white orphanage. As soon as we pulled into the driveway, a pretty white woman with a big blonde flip-up hair do, powder blue dress, and pearls materialized through the front door.

"Welcome, welcome," she said, her arms outstretched. Years later, I could hear that woman's voice when I heard Effie Trinket in the movie *The Hunger Games*.

"I'm Miss Moreland. Y'all come in and have a seat in the parlor."

As she waved us inside, the red nail polish on her fingertips flashed in the sun as though they had been dipped in blood. We entered the house, and I glanced around the foyer. It was bigger than ours and seemed more luxurious. Paintings on the walls were framed in gold, and the carpets looked soft and plush. We were directed into the parlor and sat down on the velvety chairs and settees. I heard a rumble of footsteps above, then a group of white girls descended the stairs and stood in the parlor doorway.

"Have a seat, girls," Miss Moreland said.

They settled onto seats across from us. Miss Moreland hovered in the doorway.

"Well, isn't this nice. You girls have fun," she said, then disappeared.

A cluster of eyeballs, blue and cautious, examined us. We stared back. No one tried to start a conversation. I didn't dislike these girls just because they were white, and I got the feeling that they felt the same way about us. We simply didn't have anything in common to talk about.

After a few moments of painful silence, Miss Moreland reappeared.

"Let's all go to the back yard for some refreshments."

We all followed her outside. Their orphanage had a big back yard with fruit trees and an in-ground swimming pool complete with diving board and slide. There was a table set with cookies and lemonade off to the side in the sun. We all sat down together, but one by one, the white girls got up and went into the house. They emerged some time later wearing bathing suits.

At that time, there was a legal doctrine in the United States called "Separate but Equal" which established that public facilities, housing, schools, public transportation, medical care, and jobs all had to be separated between blacks, coloreds (people of mixed races), and whites, and that each of these amenities were deemed equal. This doctrine was declared to be valid under the Equal Protection Clause in the Fourteenth Amendment of the Constitution, which guaranteed equal protection under the law to all citizens.

Trouble was, as I soon found out, almost nothing was equal. Many black kids in the all-black schools had to use old textbooks, used equipment, and were often taught by underskilled teachers. They read books written by and written about white people. Government officials required literacy tests and poll taxes, which made it next to impossible for a black man to vote. The government eventually saw the error of its ways, and the Supreme Court overturned this doctrine in 1954. Unfortunately, most of the Deep South didn't get memo.

I had heard that all the orphanages were equal, and that the white girls got no special treatment—that they had all the same things that we had. That just wasn't the case. Okay, their front lawn was neatly manicured, and so was ours. But their driveway in the front of the house was blacktopped, whereas our driveway in the back of the house was gravel. Their foyer and parlor were fancier than ours. But it wasn't until I saw their opulent back yard complete with swimming pool that the differences became crystal clear.

All afternoon, we black girls continued to sit at the table in the blazing sun sipping warm lemonade and watched the golden-pony-tail-flopping, bubble-gum-blowing white girls swim in the refreshing pool. I felt uncomfortable and confused. The air was swampy-thick and smelled like salamanders. Everything was damp through. Trees gasped for breath. I wanted to go swimming more than anything, but we weren't allowed to bathe in the same pool as the whites. In fact, we couldn't drink from the same water fountain or eat at the same restaurants or attend the same churches. We were prohibited, by law, from interacting.

Miss Moreland finally came outside and stood beside our table.

"Father is here to take y'all home," she said. "I hope you girls had a nice afternoon."

Her sticky smile latched into my skin like a fish hook. We were led out the front door and

tumbled into the station wagon. Miss Moreland waved as we backed out of the driveway.

"Did you girls have a nice afternoon?" Father smiled in the rear-view mirror.

"Yes, Father," one of the girls murmured.

I knew that Father was a good and decent man, so I found it hard to believe he could think that we would have a good time being shown our place. I stared at my lap. My hands turtled into fists, and anger rose inside me like bile.

Later that afternoon, I sat in the back yard in the shade of a tree with Frances and Maria Cuevas. Frances sat twirling a finger through her curly hair, a habit I soon found she did whenever she was out of sorts. Maria squeezed a blade of grass tightly between her thumbs, put her pursed lips to her thumbs and blew. What came out sounded more like a duck quack than a whistle.

"In a million years, I will never understand who thought that was a good idea," I said. "It seemed cruel to me. We didn't even talk with those girls. I felt like we weren't even there. One thing came of it—we were shown just how different things are. Separate but equal my eye."

"I wish I was white," Maria said. She blew against her thumbs again.

"I could have a banana split at the counter at Woolworth's. I could go to any college I wanted. No one would look at me like they're angry at me. I would be included."

"Blacks aren't supposed to be friendly with the whites," Frances said. She brought the twirled lock of hair to her mouth and chewed on it. "You think we'll get in trouble for going over there?"

"This doesn't happen in Cuba," I said. "There, if you want to mix, you mix. Here if you mix, you're thrown in jail. Or worse."

"Well," Maria tossed the blade of grass aside, "I still think it would be nice to be white. If only for a day."

In Cuba, we were all expected to be educated, to go to college and to have a profession. There in the South, I soon realized, absolutely nothing was expected of a black child, especially a female black child. It was assumed we were poor, uneducated, child-like creatures. We could run our husbands' homes and be domestic servants, but the chances of getting a higher education were all but nonexistent. And forget landing a good paying job in an office. We were expected to keep our eyes lowered and to get out of the way whenever white folks passed us on the sidewalks like a dog at the heel. As for the boys, I learned that black fathers taught their sons never to wave at passing cars, just in case a white woman was inside and should become offended. There seemed no hope of a better future. It was understood that we had to be content with the scraps that fell from the white table.

My family thought that since Mario and I were in the United States, we were given the best there was to offer. But to the Southerners, we were just plain black. I found out quickly the white folks weren't about to say, "Oh, gee, you're Cuban? Well, that's different. You go to the right in that line because you're going to get special treatment." No way no how. We were part of the many. Never seen for who we were, but what we were. Automatically considered less than. That negative perception infected like a nasty virus and seeped into the marrow. It's a harsh and lonely feeling to be thought of as different. But we were different together.

That night after everyone had gone to sleep, I laid awake circling fiery thoughts about the day in my mind. Then something gently shifted, and I listened to the rain tap the window and to the soft rattle of the girls' breathing. I had a full belly, warm clothes, a comfortable bed, and the grace of chores, lessons, and friendship, and my heart became too big for my chest. Despite the day, I knew that I was blessed. And I felt truly grateful.

Chapter TWELVE

One afternoon that summer, Sister Paulette found me in the sewing room. Sister Fabian had the unfortunate task of teaching me how to sew. More times than not, I managed to stab myself and bleed on the clothes.

"There's a letter for you," Sister Paulette said handing me an envelope.

I pushed the mending aside and took the letter. It was from Nené. I would recognize his handwriting anywhere. I ripped open the envelope and unfolded the paper.

Dear Caty,
I hope this letter finds you well. I hope you like your temporary home and that you are making friends. Mima, Lydia, and I are well. We are working very hard for us all to be together again soon. Please write to us and tell us all about New Orleans. Be a good girl.
We love you,
Nené

I took the letter up to my room and sat on my bed. I traced my fingers along Nené's inky loops and swirls. I longed for a piece of home in the letter, a sprinkle of dirt from under his nails that may have settled in the bottom of the envelope. A coffee stain on the paper. After rereading the letter, I held it to my face and breathed deeply hoping for a hint of his cologne, or the snap of his fresh linen shirtsleeve as it rested on the paper while he wrote, the smell of pork frying in the background. Anything. I folded the letter and tucked it into my pocket.

That weekend I visited Mario, and he told me that he got a letter, too. That summer, we received letters from home every week, each one ending with a promise from Nené that we would be reunited soon. I was filled with hope. When you choose to hope, odds are you'll get your heart broken, but you get back up and commit to the idea again and again, because it's worth the risk. It's the grittiness of hope that keeps you going.

But by August, the letters came less frequently, and by the end of the summer, they stopped coming altogether. A worm of doubt wriggled into my heart like a tiny crack in an heirloom. I tried keep fear from muddying my mind, but I couldn't help thinking that I might not see my family again.

I saw Mario every weekend that summer. It bothered me that he was so angry and always fighting the American boys. He was imprisoned and suffering, and there was nothing either of us could do about it. It became too painful for us to meet, so we decided it was best to give our visits a rest.

On August 15th, we celebrated the Feast of the Assumption of the Blessed Virgin Mary, which commemorates her death and assumption of her body up into heaven before it could begin to decay. On that day, all the sisters in training took their vows of poverty, chastity, and obedience.

Although we use the term "sister" and "nun" as though they mean the same thing, technically there is a difference. A Catholic nun is a woman who lives her life in contemplation in a monastery or such place that is cloistered (away from the world) or semi-cloistered. Her life consists of prayer and humble work around the monastery. She professes the perpetual solemn vows of poverty, celibacy, and obedience.

A sister, on the other hand, is a woman who lives her life out in the world ministering, and working for the good of mankind—like Mother Teresa. A sister's life is sometimes called "active" or "apostolic" because she's out in the world preaching and living the Gospel and not confined to monastery. She professes simple vows which also include vows of poverty, celibacy, and obedience. The male equivalent of a sister is called a monk or a friar.

The difference between solemn and simple vows is that a woman who takes a solemn vow of poverty renounces ownership of all worldly goods, whereas a woman who takes the simple vow still professes to poverty, but she's allowed to own property or collect on an inheritance from one's parents. They can own the property but they can't make a profit for their own financial gain. Regardless of whether one is a nun or a sister, they are both addressed as "sister."

It takes a long time to make a sister or a nun. First, a woman must qualify to start the process. She must: be Catholic, be single, not have any dependent children, not have any debts, be healthy, be between the ages of 18 and about 40. Furthermore, although a college degree is not a must, many religious orders require that a woman have at least a bachelor's degree.[24]

For those women who are brave enough, there are a number of steps she must go through to prove herself. According to the Sisters of the Holy Family of Nazareth:

First, after she declares her intentions, she will go through the Initial Discernment which is marked by a period of questioning, prayer, and reflection. After that, during the Affiliacy phase, the woman must consider the possible vocation she might want to serve.

Second, after she decides that this is the life she has chosen, the novice would receive the habit of the order. Usually it is a plain white veil. She would then go through a postulancy, or a testing period in order to live that type of lifestyle for anywhere from six months to a year.

After that, both she and the order she had chosen would determine whether they were a good fit. If all systems were a go, she would move on to the second phase where she'd take her temporary vows. That could last anywhere from one to three years. Finally, if she chose to become a nun, she would then petition to take her permanent, solemn vows.

On that day in August, we all attended the ceremony. It was really quite a sight to see. Thirty sisters floated up the center aisle all dressed in incredibly elaborate white dresses that some proud aunt or family member had created for her. The "brides of Christ" drifted past us and ascended up toward the altar. Like any good marriage, it's not over when the "I dos" are said. That's when the journey begins.

With our family being so Catholic, there was a time when I thought about becoming a sister or a nun, but after seeing their lifestyle up close, the day to day of it and all the politics, I realized I wouldn't be cut out for that kind of life. For so long I had held the image of the sisters up on a pedestal, but living with them every day, I quickly saw that they were as human as anyone else. In fact, one morning, I watched two sisters get into a fist fight in the chapel in the middle of Mass. That human outburst aside, I still hold the highest respect for anyone who has the guts to take on that responsibility.

Summer faded into fall, and Mother enrolled us new girls in school. We were entering the forest of brown paper lunch sacks, and small desks, and homework. The grammar school was about a mile from the orphanage. Father drove us to school in the beige station wagon, and since we went to different schools depending on our ages, he drove us all in shifts. The first batch left at 7:30 a.m., then the rest of us left at 8:30 a.m.

Frances and I attended the all-black Catholic grammar school run by the Sisters of the Blessed Sacrament whose Order's sole purpose was to educate black children. Sister Stella was our teacher. She was a tall, thin white woman with a beautiful face who for some reason never smiled. It was as though she wore a mask, because she showed no expression whatsoever. She was never mean or angry. She just seemed joyless.

Vivian and Maria attended the Catholic white school. I was happy for Maria, because I knew how important it was for her to feel special in the eyes of the white folks. She had always longed to be white, like a white cloud in the sky, full of nothingness.

They had started to integrate schools in New Orleans a few years before I arrived. On November 16, 1960, three six-year-old black girls,

Leona Tate, Tessie Prevost, and Gail Etienne, began first grade at the all-white school McDonogh No. 19. The girls were nicknamed The McDonogh Three. All the white parents promptly removed their children from McDonogh.

On that same day across town, another six-year-old girl named Ruby Bridges was escorted into the all-white William Frantz Elementary School accompanied by three U.S. Marshalls. That event was commemorated by Norman Rockwell in his painting titled *The Problem We All Live With.* By the end of the week, only three white children remained in William Frantz, and they were forbidden from interacting with Ruby. Only one woman, Barbara Henry from Boston, Massachusetts agreed to teach Ruby, and for over a year, she taught her alone in the classroom.

Each morning, a group of about forty white women known as the "cheerleaders" lined the streets and sidewalks shouting violent and racist threats at little Ruby as she came to school. They held placards that read things like "Race Mixing is Communism" and "We Want to Keep Our School White" and "Integration is a Mortal Sin" and "God Demands Segregation."

God demands segregation. What a load of crap. I'm offended when people use God as an excuse to further their own agenda. God has nothing to do with it. In my mind, there are only four words that a true Christian ever needs as a guide to live by: What. Would. Jesus. Do? I can't imagine that Jesus, even on his worst day, with a bad case of Jewfro, teenage acne, an abscessed tooth, or explosive diarrhea would ever utter the words "God demands segregation."

If we Americans were to actually live by the teachings of Jesus, we would have universal health care, no death penalty, no discrimination based on race, religion, lack of religion, gender, or sexual orientation. Men and women would get equal pay, the wealthy would help pay for the poor, and everyone would love their neighbor as themselves. Dare to dream.

Chapter THIRTEEN

Since we all went to Catholic schools, we all had to wear uniforms. The first afternoon we came back to the orphanage from school, we raced upstairs, wild as fall leaves, slipped out of our uniforms, and we Cuban girls let them float to the floor. My mother never taught me to hang up my clothes or put them away, and apparently neither did Vivian's, Maria's or Frances'. We never knew to do that. Sister Paulette found us in the back yard.

"Catalina, Maria, Frances, and Vivian, come inside the house at once."

We followed her inside and up to our room. She pointed to the uniforms on the floor.

"This is not where they go. You are to hang up your uniforms and keep your rooms tidy. Is that understood?"

The following day was a brilliant Indian Summer day. Warm flecks of light dripped in shafts through the tree branches as we skipped home. We dashed upstairs, quickly got into our play clothes and headed to the back yard to play. A few minutes later, Sister Paulette exploded out the back door. Her face was pinched, and her mouth puckered into a thin line like an angry doll. She stormed across the yard toward us. She was carrying a wooden paddle. She stood beside Vivian.

"Perhaps I didn't make myself clear."

She drew back her arm like Babe Ruth swinging for the fence and let her have it. Vivian crumpled to the ground. The rest of the girls stopped and stared. I was dumbfounded and froze in my tracks, that is, until I saw Sister turn and face me. Her nostrils flared and her eyes narrowed, and she headed my way. I raced for my life toward the back door, but Sister was faster. She clobbered me with the paddle across the back of my knees, and I faceplanted into the grass. I laid there motionless, hoping she'd think I was dead. From different parts of the back yard, I heard screams and thrumps as her paddle connected with flesh. Finally, she came back and stood over me.

"Now, when I tell you to hang up your uniforms, I hope you understand that I mean it."

Vivian, Maria, Frances, and I hobbled upstairs and hung up our uniforms. I had never been spanked or struck in the whole of my life, and I didn't plan to have that lesson repeated. I think Sister Paulette's methods were extreme, but from that day forward, I hung up my uniform and made sure my bed was made before I left the house.

Every day, Vivian, Maria, Frances, and I walked home from school. At one part near the highway, the sidewalk dipped down through a dark tunnel below the road—a bottle-littered stretch that was dank and stunk of pee. One afternoon as we entered the blackened tunnel mouth, a truck with several white boys crawled up beside us and slowed down. I sensed a wrongness about the situation, an Edgar Cayce way of seeing bad before it happened. The boys were drinking beer. One of them leaned out of the window.

"Well, hello, ladies," the boy said with a smile.

"Hello."

"It's a fine afternoon for a stroll."

"Yes, it is," Maria said.

Just then, he snorted air through his nose, rattled a loogie in his throat, and hocked it at us. Of all people, Maria was the one it hit. The boys sped off laughing, drinking their beer, smug and indifferent.

I felt pure rage, for the inhumanity and the indecency, but most of all, for the shattered look I saw on Maria's face. We were all momentarily duped into thinking that whites and blacks were on a level playing field—that we could exchange courteous banter about the weather. We were again reminded of our place. I wanted so badly to believe in the good of people, but anger squatted inside me and its tendrils slithered their way into my heart and bones. It was incidents like this, repeated over and over, that made it difficult to trust. Each negative encounter hardened me bit by bit, like a snail laying down fresh coats of protein and minerals to create its shell. They became bricks in the wall.

One afternoon, Mother Clement Marie spied me sitting alone in the playroom. She adjusted her crutches and dragged her worrisome misshapen legs across the room and settled onto a chair beside me.

"What thoughts are swimming in that head of yours?" I told her what had happened—about the white boys spitting on Maria.

"That's just how things are. It isn't fair. It just is. You need to rise above."

Mother Clement Marie was able to shuffle off her mortal coil, and I know she wanted to teach me to let that badness roll like water off a duck's back. I didn't understand that at the time. To me, it seemed as though she took what I told her in stride, as if I was making too big a deal out of what had happened. And it was a big deal to me. I could still see those boys riding off, their wide smiles and hard white eyes, crinkled by laughter.

No matter how much truth there was in Mother's words, I couldn't rid myself of that experience. Even days later, I only had to close my eyes and that awful day would come creeping back from the shadow of my mind whispering "It ain't over. That badness is here to stay." Understanding one's place was heavy knowledge, and I didn't know if I could ever make my throat large enough to swallow what the whites were shoveling.

They say that the Civil Rights Movement sang its way to freedom, and that the Blues was born from pain. We had a small choir at the orphanage directed by Sister Helena. She loved to sing and taught anyone who was interested in music how to sing, too.

That week, I spent my afternoons after school in the dark chapel listening to Sister Helena practice her music. I'd stretch my back against the hard, wooden pew and listen to the organ cough up notes as her foot scraped across the floor pedals. By the end of the week, I decided to join the choir. I suppose I joined because of the frustration and the choke of anger I couldn't shake. As soon as I started to sing, something shifted. I discovered the power of music to unfasten the grip of fury and touch an untouchable place deep inside with its soothing balm.

Chapter **FOURTEEN**

Every fall, Tulane University gave our orphanage tickets for all their home games and donated a bus to take us there and back. We sat in the black section with the other black folks and cheered on the home team. The boys home was given tickets to the games as well, so I was able to see Mario. One afternoon, he and I sat together for a while at the game. There was a pleasant chill in the air, and huge puff-white clouds were frozen in the deep blue sky as though they had been thumbtacked there.

"I'd like to go to college here one day," I said.

"To study? Dream on."

"I want to be a lawyer, or maybe work for the United Nations. I want to help children all over the world who don't have families."

He shook his head.

"I don't see why I can't someday."

"I'll give you two words why you can't. Jim. Crow."

Jim Crow was a stock character, a stereotypically lazy, foolish black good-for-nothing that cropped up in minstrel shows that made the rounds in the South during the mid-nineteenth century. From the mid-1870s to the mid-1960s, the term Jim Crow came to symbolize the laws and practices of segregation and discrimination against black people.[25] During that time, derogatory symbols, advertisements and cartoons were circulated which only served to reinforce the white idea that blacks were inferior—somehow subhuman.[26] It allowed the whites to justify not letting blacks vote, be educated, hold meaningful jobs, or live in white neighborhoods. The Jim Crow South and its laws were meant to reinforce white supremacy in every way and real threat to the blacks' lives.

The Union victory in the Civil War may have given slaves their freedom in 1865, but whites in the South—along with white groups like the Ku Klux Klan—weren't about to give up their supremacy without a fight. In an attempt to reverse those black rights and freedoms, new segregation laws called "black codes" were implemented. These codes regulated and restricted the movement of slaves reinstating the antebellum Southern social order in which whites occupied a higher social rung than blacks. Black codes limited black life in so many ways. They determined the types of businesses African Americans could own and the time of day they could visit downtown. They stipulated that no more than three African Americans could ever gather together in one place. It gave the whites legal authority over blacks when no police officer was present. Louisiana passed one of the first laws officially striping blacks of the right to register to vote.[27] Basically, everything that could be segregated in Louisiana was: restaurants, hotels, street cars, jails, cemeteries even churches. Even the children had separate playgrounds and amusement parks. Interaction between blacks and white all but disappeared.

Not coincidently, lynchings increased dramatically. Usually carried out by a mob, lynchings were violent and public acts of torture that traumatized black people throughout the country. State and local officials turned a blind eye. Most victims of lynchings were either publically hung or shot, but some were castrated, beaten, dismembered or burned at the stake. They were often advertised in newspapers beforehand so photographers could arrive early and set up their equipment. Afterward, the photographer sold the photos or printed them up as souvenir postcards.[28]

The threat of violence was a way to keep blacks in line and reinforce white supremacy. Whites could attack blacks and not get in trouble with the law. There wasn't much the blacks could do because the police, prosecutors, judges, and juries were all white.

All lynchings were horrific, but the worst were the public spectacle lynchings. These were large spectator events that drew crowds sometimes numbering in the thousands, where souvenirs of body parts were often sold, alongside postcards and other mementos. One of the most gruesome I had ever read about was the lynching of Luther Holbert and his wife in 1904 in Doddville, Mississippi. They had been accused of killing a wealthy white planter. Whether that accusation was true or not, we'll never know, because there was no trial. Both victims were tied to a tree and forced to hold out their hands while members of the mob methodically chopped off their fingers one by one and distributed them as souvenirs. Next, their ears were cut off. Mr. Holbert was then beaten so severely that his skull was fractured and one of his eyes was left hanging from its socket. Members of the mob used a large corkscrew to bore holes into the victims' bodies and pull large chunks of 'quivering flesh,' after which both victims were thrown onto a raging fire and burned.[29] The white men, women, and children present watched the horrific event while enjoying deviled eggs, lemonade, and whiskey in a picnic-like atmosphere. According to the Tuskegee Institute's records by state and by race from 1882 to 1968, there have been a total of 4743 lynchings.[30]

Despite the constant threat of terror, little by little, brave men and women stood up for their rights and declared enough was enough. What they did those days had an effect, not only on those of that time, but also on children that had not been born. Homer Plessy, a New Orleans shoemaker who was 1/8th African American and could pass for white, in 1892 purchased a first-class train ticket and sat in the whites only railcar and refused to leave.[31] Black soldiers returning home from WWII demanded the same rights as whites for faithfully serving their country. In 1955, Rosa Parks refused to give up her seat to a white man on a bus. In 1963, Martin Luther King, Jr, delivered his moving *I Have a Dream* speech. Like a pebble dropped into a pond, each courageous act of defiance rippled out and multiplied—leading to the fall of the Jim Crow laws.

Although, thank the blessed Lord, blacks no longer live under the threat of being lynched, an argument can be made that "lynchings" haven't really stopped, but that the different types of punishment have gone from hangings to incarcerations, stop and frisk, racial profiling, and police killing of innocents. These acts might not be intended to reinforce white supremacy as they were in the days of Jim Crow, nevertheless, they continue to instill fear in the black communities.

While in New Orleans, I could see the rumble of change. The year before I came, Tulane had still refused to admit black students—that is until two black women challenged the University's rules. Barbara Marie Guillory and Pearlie Hardin Elloie applied for admission in April 1961. Elloie received a rejection letter that said the university would approve her application and allow her to attend if they didn't think it would be illegal to do so. Ms. Guillory received a similar rejection letter. They both sued the university and won.[32] Brick by brick, the walls were coming down.

We saw victories like these, but we saw the setbacks, too. On October 10th, the Cuban community in New Orleans celebrated the commemoration of Carlos Manuel de Céspedes and his famous *"El Grito de Yara,"* or "Cry of the Yara" marking the start of the First Cuban War of Independence.

Céspedes was an important figure to us Cubans. Born in Bayamo, Cuba on April 18, 1819, Céspedes was educated in Havana before travelling to Spain where he received his law degree. He joined the Army under General D. Juan Prim. After their defeat, he traveled Europe and eventually returned to Bayamo, Cuba, where he set up his law practice and became active once more in politics. Unfortunately, because of his anti-Spanish views, he was arrested and told to leave Bayamo. He organized a war for independence in Oriente province. He reminded the people that they needed to fight because for centuries, they had done nothing to fight against Spanish rule for more than three centuries.[33] On October 10, 1868, the first war for Cuban independence began when Céspedes delivered his historic *"Grito de Yara"* speech at his sugar mill *La Demajagua* declaring war on Spain, beginning the Ten Years' War.[34]

Señora De La Vega was a tutor assigned to us Cuban girls by Mr. Ramos. She was a beautiful Cuban woman with olive skin, green eyes and black hair pulled tightly into a bun. She came to the orphanage Monday through Friday after school. We sat at the dining room table while she drilled us in math, history, and science. One afternoon, she arrived with a handful of colorful brochures.

"I have good news," she said. "I've made arrangements for you girls to attend this year's commemoration of Carlos Manuel de Céspedes. As Cubans, it's important for you to never forget where you come from." She passed out the brochures. "Take the bus after school Wednesday afternoon to City Hall and meet me there."

So, that Wednesday, we boarded a bus to City Hall and stood in line. As we inched toward the front door, a few white adults approached us. Their name tags read that they were members of the administration at City Hall. I thought because we were Cuban she might escort us inside ahead of the others.

"I'm going to have to ask you girls to leave," one of the adults said.

"We're here for the commemoration," I said.

"I can't let you in."

"But we're Cuban. Señora De La Vega has our tickets at the door."

"No blacks are allowed at the commemoration. I'm sorry, but you have to leave now."

As we skulked passed the white people in line, I could feel their stare. It was humiliating. I kept my eyes on the sidewalk until we reached the bus stop. We wordlessly boarded the bus and headed back to the orphanage.

The following afternoon, Señora De La Vega stormed into the parlor. She dropped her purse on the dining room table and sighed.

"I am more than disappointed in you girls. After all I did to get those tickets for you. Do you know, the Cubans waited for your girls, but you never showed, so they continued the commemoration without you. What do you have to say for yourselves?"

"We did come." I said. "We were there in line, but when we got near the door, they told us no blacks were allowed in. We told them you were expecting us, but no one would listen. They told us we had to leave."

She shook her head and sat down. "I wish someone had told me. If we had known that, we would have cancelled the commemoration and left in order to show our solidarity."

She reached across the table and grasped our hands. "I'm sorry this happened to you."

The irony was that immediately after Céspedes' "*Grito de Yara*" speech, he freed his personal slaves, wrote a manifesto demanding complete independence from Spain, and he demanded the indemnified emancipation of all slaves everywhere. And we weren't allowed in to celebrate his commemoration because we were black.

Chapter FIFTEEN

"Try this on," Sister Fabien said. She handed me a colorful dress and a hat.

"What is it?"

"It's your Halloween costume."

"What's Halloween?"

The sisters were great at teaching us the human anatomy. Periods and pregnancy, yes. Holidays, not so much.

"Halloween is a holiday where you dress up in silly or scary costumes and people give you candy."

"They give you candy. For free?"

"Yes."

I was never one to like putting on costumes, but if dressing up meant free candy, I was first in line. Father gave us each a plastic pumpkin bucket and led us down the street. He gathered us together on the sidewalk in front of the first house.

"Now, for those of you that are new to this holiday, you go up and knock on the door then say 'Trick or Treat,' and they'll give you candy."

I had no idea what he meant by *trickortreat*, but I followed the girls to the door. I held out my arm and watched in utter amazement as a candy bar dropped into my bucket. After our buckets were filled, Father piled us into the station wagon and drove to the cemetery. He put the car in park in front of a crypt and turned to face us.

"Halloween or All Hallows' Eve falls on the evening before All Saints' Day on November 1st. It's a night when you get candy, but it's also a time to remember the dead."

He glanced out the window, and his eyes swept from side to side.

Large oak trees stood sentinel over the graves. Their branches draped in Spanish moss that flowed in the air like ghosts, like Harry Potter Dementors. The only sound we heard was the car heater wheezing. He leaned in closer and lowered his voice. "They say tonight is a special night, because the spirits are able to walk the earth." He leaned over the steering wheel and scanned the skies. "If you look really closely, you might even see a spirit."

We all gaped out the window and scoured the skies and the stone angels and lichen-covered graves, waiting to see a spirit float by the car. Just then, Father honked the horn. We all screamed then cried with laughter. He started the car and headed home. I never really believed in spirits roaming the earth, but I rubbed the goosebumps from my arms just the same.

In the fall, pecans dropped from the trees in the back yard, and we would collect them for Aunt Rose to make pecan pie. By autumn, my chores shifted to kitchen duty. I had no interest in learning how to cook, but I liked being in the warm kitchen just the same. Aunt Rose was a good and mindful cook. Some people cook simply to put food on the table. But some, like Aunt Rose, cooked with love. As soon as she returned from the grocery store, she rinsed the fruits and vegetables and arranged them in bowls. She plucked the eggs from the cardboard carton and washed them one-by-one and carefully placed them in a wire basket. After I finished cleaning and drying the breakfast dishes, Aunt Rose was already at the stove standing over a pot of soup, stirring away the day.

Mima cooked with love, too. She used to say, if you cook with anger in your heart, the food will feel it. The rice will stay undercooked not matter how long you keep it on the fire. The rare times that happened, Mima would add milk, sugar, cinnamon sticks and vanilla to make *arroz con leche*, but the rice still crunched.

The sisters would break out sweaters, scarves and thick leggings for us to wear. In Havana, I thought it was cold when the weather dropped to 65 degrees. I had no idea what cold was. I remember playing outside, and in one cold blast of wind, my body was so cold. My cheeks burned, and my hands prickled with pain as though I had pushed over a fire ant hill. I started to cry and went inside. I learned that for me, being too hot is much better than being too cold. Once my ears and feet got cold, I could never get warm. I remember seeing snow for the first time and thinking how beautiful and peaceful it was, watching the cottony flakes float to the ground. I still love to see the first flakes of snow fall—through the window of my nice warm house.

That fall, I caught a very bad flu. At one point, they brought Mario over to visit with me—not because they thought I was going to die. They just thought he might cheer me up. And he did.

I remember when I was sick in Cuba, it was Nené who cared for me. He sat beside my bed, fed me and read to me. Those long days and nights while I was isolated in the orphanage infirmary, Mother Clement Marie came and sat with me every chance she got. In the evenings, she came and gave me my medicine. I know she was a busy woman, but it meant the world to me that she took the time to sit with me. It made me feel wanted and loved. She was put on the earth to bring light into darkness.

It never occurred to me that mother was handicapped. Many different Sisters and Brothers visited our orphanage to attend daily Mass, visit or tutor us in the summer. I sometimes catch them trying not to watch her shuffle across the room to her seat, face pinched in pain. She never uttered a howl or even a whimper. Once she got to where she needed to go, she'd collapse in the chair with a sigh and unfastened the grips of her arm crutches and prop them against the wall or the back of the chair. I didn't notice until they noticed. She knew that her crippled body made some people squirm, but she never pretended that she wasn't lame or suffering. She owned it, which made me admire her more.

Mother Clement Marie loved us all like a mamma lion. I had grown so close to her that I never wanted to disappoint her. Clemency means mercy, and time and time again, that's just what she showed me. Admittedly, I sometimes misbehaved, and yet she never used a paddle on me. Instead, she had a way of disciplining without raising her voice. She looked at me a certain way and talked to me, and I would start crying. You could call her the "Catalina Whisperer." With just one look, I would stop whatever I was doing and would sit next to her. I loved that woman with my whole heart.

I was finally strong enough to come downstairs for Thanksgiving dinner. I had no idea what that holiday was all about, but I dressed for dinner with the rest of the girls and joined them in the dining room. The sisters had replaced our smaller tables with one massive linen-draped table that ran the length of the room. It was elegantly set with china and silverware—real silver, and glass goblets that glowed like jewels by the light of the candles. We could have been dining at Kensington Palace. The table was loaded with decorative bowls filled with vegetables, baskets of homemade rolls and a platter that cupped an enormous turkey. I had to hand it to them, when those Sisters cranked it up, they cranked it up. It was all so delicious, except for the pumpkin pie. I had never had apples until I came to this country. I quickly found out that I love apple pie with vanilla ice cream. That wretched pumpkin pie tasted like paste to me. I imagine it's an acquired taste, one that I have yet to acquire. I'll stick with apple pie a la mode, thank you very much.

Chapter SIXTEEN

Pete finally came to New Orleans to visit us. Mario and I received letters and phone calls from him, but this was the first time since we left Cuba that I saw him. On that Saturday morning in December, I put on the prettiest dress from the rack and waited for him, shaky kneed, staring out the front parlor window for what seemed like a hundred years.

Suddenly, a bus pulled up over across the street and stopped. I saw him get off the bus and cross the street to come to the orphanage. He wore a crisp U.S. Army uniform. I ran through the front door, down the porch steps and jumped into his arms. He held me so tightly. To see Pete's smile after all that time, to feel his arms lift me, and to smell his clean skin—that feeling was indescribable. Whenever he lifted me in his arms back home, I was careful not to squeeze him too tightly so as not to wrinkle his cassock. Rumpling his uniform was the furthest thing from my mind. I clung to his neck like a drowning man grips a lifesaver and started sobbing. Just then, I noticed that Mario was with him, and he was crying too.

"How did you get out of Cuba?" I asked.

He set me down and wiped the tears from my cheek.

"A few of my friends and I made it to the Uruguayan Embassy, then we traveled to Mexico. We stayed there for a few weeks, then I crossed into the United States and joined the Army. I have a feeling the United States is going to invade Cuba, and when it does, I want to be on the right side fighting Fidel. But now, I'm here. I told you I'd come for you."

A thrill pulsed through me. "Are we leaving with you now?"

"Not yet, but soon. I'm working on getting Nené, Lydia and Mima out first."

I took his hand and led him and Mario into the orphanage. I introduced them to Father, the sisters and some of the girls. I watched Pete speak with Mother Clement Marie. The way they smiled at each other and laughed, I could immediately tell there was a shared admiration.

After their visit, Pete, Mario and I went for a walk. Sister Paulette insisted that Elaine Lugo come along as my chaperone. I have no idea why she thought it necessary for me to be escorted with my own brothers, but she did. Elaine was one of two older girls who lived at the orphanage and attended college. I remember thinking that day how beautiful Elaine was and how handsome Pete was in his olive uniform. Mario and I walked behind them, and I noticed them glance at each other, and he smiled at her. I had seen him aim that smile at a girl a thousand times, but this one was different. It was warm, like light through colored glass. Something unseen between them shimmered. Their stolen glances were weighted with unspoken words. I wondered if I would ever find someone someday to look at me that way. Pete bent his tall frame down to meet Elaine's and whispered something. Their heads bowed together, heart-shaped, as they spoke.

The sun sparkled through the tree branches casting little jewels of light against the sidewalk. We moseyed our way to the movies, and afterward with ice cream cones in hand, started back toward the orphanage.

"Follow me." Pete ran toward a photo booth. He pulled the curtain back and jerked his head. "Get in, you two."

Mario and I ducked into the booth and sat down. Pete rolled a few coins into the slot and we flashed our ice creamy mugs at the flash. Pete scanned the strip of pictures.

"Mima will love these."

We returned to the orphanage and climbed the porch steps.

"Be good," he said with a hug. "I'll be back soon."

I gave him a sticky kiss on the neck and backed my way inside the front door, not wanting to release him from my gaze—as a man dying of thirst beholds a glass of water. Once inside, I ran to the parlor window and parted the curtains. I watched as Mario and Pete boarded the bus and disappeared around the corner.

After that day, I knew that Mother Clement Marie saw me differently. She never said it, but I felt as though she admired me a bit more. It wasn't anything I did or said. I think she was impressed with Pete, and luckily, that feeling trickled down to me.

In the weeks leading up to Christmas, we decorated the house with ribbons and red and white poinsettia plants and silver garland and fresh pine boughs. Trays of frosted cookies and stripity candy magically appeared on the coffee table on movie night. Children from different schools visited our orphanage and sang carols to us. Musicians and singers from Motown volunteered to perform for us, too. Tulane hosted a Christmas party for us on their campus, and the students gave each of us a gift. I had never experienced such joy—what Mother Clement Marie called the Christmas spirit.

Mrs. Sheffield was a friend to the sisters at the orphanage. She was nice to all the girls, but occasionally, she invited me over to her house for afternoon tea. She was a light-skinned black woman with straightened black hair that flipped up into a curl at her neck. She was a teacher at the local high school. I'm not sure why she singled me out, but she did, and I was grateful for the break.

While sipping tea at her dining room table one of those afternoons, Mrs. Sheffield drew deeply on her cigarette and glanced down at my feet.

"Catalina, those shoes look too small for your feet."

"They're good shoes, ma'am," I said. "They still have a lot of wear in 'em."

"Do your feet hurt?"

"At first, but then as I wear them, I get used to it."

She placed her teacup onto the saucer and crushed her cigarette out in the glass ashtray at her elbow. "Get your coat. We're going shopping."

"That's not necessary, ma'am."

"Pish posh. Get in the car."

We drove to Maison Blanche and meandered through rows and rows of loafers, Mary Janes, high heels and boots. She finally pointed to a pair of the most beautiful Wizard-of-Oz-ruby-red-slipper shoes I had ever seen in my life. As the shoe salesman slipped them onto my feet, I lost the ability to speak. Mrs. Sheffield smiled at me, yet addressed the salesman.

"We'll take them."

I shook my head, but she raised her palm to me. "I insist. Merry Christmas, Catalina."

She dropped my too-small shoes in the shopping bag and let me wear my shiny new shoes right there and then. I loved the clickety sound of my heels on the store's tiled floors mixed in with the Christmas Musak.

Mrs. Sheffield drove me home, and as we walked in the house, Sister Paulette lowered her eyes.

"What's this?"

"Oh, Sister, I took Catalina shopping."

Sister smiled at us, and made polite small talk for a few minutes, but as soon as the front door closed behind Mrs. Sheffield, that smile drooped as though her face had been greased.

"Take those off. They look ridiculous."

"She bought them for me, for Christmas."

She pushed me down onto the floor and pulled the ruby shoes from my feet. "You won't be wearing any hoity-toity shoes in this house. You need to know your place in this world, and that means living a life that is disciplined and humble. The sooner you learn that, the better off you'll be."

I sat on the floor and watched her walk away with my pretty red shoes. I never saw them again, but I never forgot them either. And I never forgot how she tried to get me to think of myself like the white folks did—like I was inferior, and that I needed to know my place in the world.

A determination covered my body like a thick blanket. My blood became hot and moved in all directions. Right then and there on that floor, I made a promise to myself. I was going to study hard and succeed at whatever I wanted to do, no matter what it took and no matter what anyone thought. And one day, I would buy myself a pair of flashy red shoes.

Chapter SEVENTEEN

There came a knock on the door on Christmas Eve night, and a big fat white man in a red velvet suit and long white beard entered. The girls cheered and ran to greet him, but I shadowed behind Father Coffey.

"Don't be afraid, Catalina," he said. "It's Santa Claus."

"I don't know this man. We've never met."

Father led me toward the door, and that fat man let out a ho-hoey laugh that shook the windows. I ducked behind Father again.

"Santa Claus comes once a year on Christmas Eve to give good little boys and girls presents," Father explained.

"Why?"

"It's just what he does."

Christmas wasn't really big in our culture. We decorated a small tree in the living room and set up a Nativity scene or a crèche on a card table in the corner. Typically, people didn't work from December 18th to January 10th, because that time was spent with the family.

On Christmas Eve, or *Noche Buena*, we ate roasted pig, although because we lived in the city, we didn't roast it ourselves. We bought our Christmas pig already roasted. People who lived in the country dug a pit in their yards, filled it with banana leaves and coals and lowered the prepared pig into the pit where it roasted all day. Family and friends gathered around the pit throughout the day. Children played in the yard, and the adults listened to music, drank cocktails, and smoked cigars. In the evening when the pig was finally done, they all feasted.

On January 6th, we celebrated the Epiphany commemorating the night that the Three Kings found the baby Jesus in the manger.

Although in Matthew's Gospel, the only Book to refer to the Magi, he never mentions exactly how many wise men came and what their names were. Tradition in Western Christianity says that there were three wise men and that one of them, Balthasar, was black, and that they presented the Christ child with gifts. For that reason, we Cubans exchange gifts on Epiphany and not on Christmas. For us, Christmas was a holiday for the family, New Year's Eve was for the adults, and Three Kings was for the children. I respect the custom of Christmas, but for me, Three Kings holds the most meaning.

The sisters made each of us girls a special dress for Christmas. On Christmas Eve, we all attended Midnight Mass. On Christmas morning, we raced downstairs and found that we each had presents under the Christmas tree. That first year, Mother Clement Marie gave me a camera. We spent the morning ripping wrapping paper and playing with our new toys. Then we cleaned ourselves up and put on the fine dresses that the sisters had made for us, because that was the day that many of the parents came to visit their daughters. One by one, the girls were picked up and taken out somewhere.

I watched the girls wait quietly for their parents in the front parlor with pinched faces and bounce-nervous knees. I was very grateful that my family was away. I knew that they were trying to leave Cuba in order for us all to be together again, and that Mario and I had not been abandoned. That made all the difference. I watched the girls leave for the afternoon with their parents only to be deposited on the front porch that night. Many of them cried themselves to sleep. I never spoke to any of them about how they felt. It didn't seem right to cross that line. And they didn't offer their thoughts. We silently swept it under the rug and got on with life.

After the holidays, we went back to school. Winter loosened its fingers just enough to let a little warmth slip in. One morning, Aunt Rose and the sisters came into the dining room carrying several ringed cakes with purple, green and gold icing.

"What's that?" I asked Martha.

"It's the King Cake! It's delicious!"

"It's tradition," Sister Fabian said. "Some places celebrate the Three Wise Men bringing the Christ Child gifts only on Epiphany. We here in New Orleans celebrate the Three Kings from Epiphany until Shrove Tuesday or Mardi Gras. The colors of the icing have special meaning—the purple symbolizes justice, the green symbolizes faith, and the gold symbolizes power. These three colors honor the Three Kings."

The sisters placed slices of the cake on plates and passed them down the table. Martha impatiently picked the piece up in her hands, closed her eyes, and took a bite. I followed her lead and ate the cake with my hands. The light heavenly dough was soft and sweet like a twisted cinnamon roll.

"I got it," Elaine Lugo said waving her hand in the air.

I gave Martha a look.

"They bake a small figurine of the baby Jesus into the cake. Whoever gets it, gets good luck that year. It also means she has to buy next year's cakes."

Each of the nine days before Ash Wednesday, we celebrated Mardi Gras. The weekend days were spent almost entirely at the parades. Our orphanage had our own viewing stand right on one of the main streets. Of course, it was located in the black area, but that didn't matter to me. We sat on the edge of the riser and passed around slices of King Cake. I licked the icing from my piece of cake and took in the cheering crowds and the colorful floats and the festive energy.

Just then, I heard a scream, and all the sweetest of the morning instantly soured. I peeked through the risers and saw two white policemen beating a young black boy with their night sticks. The unarmed boy was huddled up on the ground, but the police continued to kick him and club him in the back and on his head. Blood smears reddened the ground.

I looked back up at the adults on the risers, and no one seemed to notice what was going on. I yanked the sleeve of the woman next to me.

"Look at what the police are doing to that boy," I said. "We have to do something."

"That's none of our business. Look away."

"What? No. That boy needs our help."

She grabbed my arm hard and spun me around. "I said turn around. That's not our affair."

I remember watching the movie *To Kill a Mockingbird*, which had been released in December 1962. That movie magnified the black experience for me. Like a camera lens coming into focus, everything suddenly made sense to me. I didn't read the novel for a long time after that, because I wanted to keep that fear, violence, and abuse at bay. There was so much day-to-day anxiety just for being black. For blacks in the South, it was a hard world of broken glass and stone. The fact was a black person never knew when they would be berated, abused, night sticked, or shot to death. The possibility of badness befalling at any moment was a constant buzz, like the sizzle-charged air just before a lightning strike.

There was so much turmoil in Cuba—not knowing who would report you to the government for God only knows what "offense." People were shot dead or hauled off to prison or plain disappeared. In New Orleans, I felt the same type of apprehension. Being black meant you had to have your antennae up at all times, looking for trouble, giving no one a reason to mistreat you. Even then, there were no guarantees.

I came to understand that if a black person in the South didn't mind their Ps and Qs, he or she could be killed. Just because. That was a fact. That boy was getting the life beaten out of him, and no one came to his rescue. We were just supposed to sit there and enjoy the parade. It was madness. I wanted to do something, but I didn't know what to do. I felt so ashamed, but the truth was, I was too afraid to speak up. Fear holds fast what can't be said. I tried to focus my eyes forward on the parade, but the floats drifted past in a water-colored blur, and the crowd noises and music all died away. The only sound I heard came from the police below the riser. One of them grunted each time he kicked that poor boy. Years later, the memory of that sound came flooding back when I heard similar grunts while watching a professional tennis player backhand a ball. I glanced once more under the riser. The boy no longer made any noise. He lay starfished and unconscious on the ground. As the police gripped his heels and dragged the bloodied boy away, I turned back toward the parade. I lifted my eyes and watched an airplane scratch a long white scar across the blue sky.

I know Mother Clement Marie told me that was just how things were, that life wasn't fair, and I needed to rise above. But all those explanations of why I should shut up and accept the unjust white rules, why I had to sit in the back of the bus, or why I had to drink at a different water fountain, or why blacks in general were treated with such disregard—those explanations just weren't sinking in. I couldn't bring myself to understand, but the fear penetrated me anyway, absorbed into my very being. Years later, it's still a fear that I carry. I can be very social, but in the presence of someone in a position of authority, I become very cautious and unsure of myself.

Even now as an adult, I sometimes find myself crippled with fear and become very standoffish. Whether in the work environment or in my personal life, whenever I encounter a situation that's even remotely competitive, I back off. I know it may not make sense, but I get that gut feeling that any conflict can devolve into a life or death struggle. That fear, however irrational, has kept me from applying for certain jobs and has hindered me from experiencing my full potential. Without those formative experiences, I would have been fearless in my professional life. In private, I'm confident. But not in the workplace where I am in a subordinate role. That triggers a feeling of intense fear for me that I cannot for the life of me overcome. I wish it was different, but as Mother Clement Marie said, that's just how things are.

I never did find out what happened to that boy underneath the risers, but I learned two additional hard lessons that day at the parade: I have to be very careful around the police, and I could never trust them completely.

Chapter EIGHTEEN

With the exception of Lydia's *quinceañera*, our family never celebrated birthdays. The Catholic Church doesn't frown on celebrating birthdays. In fact, the mass itself is called a celebration. I think Mima thought that any kind of adulation beyond honoring the mass was unnecessary and frivolous.

At the beginning of each month, Aunt Rose baked a birthday cake to celebrate those girls' birthdays that fell in that month. In March of 1963, I turned ten years old, and I shared my first birthday cake with one other girl. After dinner, Father dimmed the dining room lights, and a few of the sisters carried in a big cake with white icing and pink sugar roses. The candle glow lifted up onto all the smiling faces and cast faint circles of light that flickered and swayed like an aurora borealis across the dark ceiling. When I heard my name sung, my insides flooded with happiness, and it flowed out my eyes and down my cheeks. I've celebrated many birthdays since then, but I'll never forget that very first birthday.

During Holy Week that year, a different African American woman took me shopping at Maison Blanche for my Easter outfit. After the fancy red shoe incident, I was no longer invited to visit Mrs. Sheffield. I missed her and our afternoon teas. That new woman, whose name I never knew, bought me a hat, gloves, dress, socks, and shoes. She was skinny and a bit bow legged. Her clothes weren't as fashionable as Mrs. Sheffield's, and she wasn't as refined in manner. She seemed to be a gentle, plain, and humble woman. If I had to guess, I'd say she wasn't far from falling on hard times herself, nevertheless, she paid for everything.

As a reminder of Mrs. Sheffield's and the plain woman's generosity to me, every year I make sure to buy a little something nice for myself to wear for Easter, and I say a silent, heartfelt prayer for those selfless women who made me feel so special.

After Easter morning mass, we piled into three cars and Father and Sisters Paulette and Fabian drove us to the city park to an Easter egg hunt. We joined the boys and girls already assembled on the park lawn with its new grass, all damp and green, each blade stretching its arms up toward the sky after its long slumber. Butterflies fluttered drunkenly from one new blossom to the next. Birds sang their fresh-peeled song. Women handed out small Easter baskets to us. A middle-aged man was check-check-checking a bullhorn. He wore thick glasses and a grey Fedora hat with a yellow feather in the band. He held up a stop watch.

"Welcome," the man said into a bullhorn. "I'm Mr. Johnson. Can I have y'all gather together in groups by age. These nice ladies will assist the partners to help the youngest children. Then we need a group of children here from ages six to twelve. The teenagers will stand over here.

"As you can see, we've hidden eggs throughout the grounds," he said. "Most are the hard-boiled colored kind. But there are a few that are plastic which open and reveal a special prize. There's also one golden egg. Whoever finds that egg gets a special prize. Also, the one with the most eggs gets a prize."

We shuffled from foot to foot in anticipation. We could see that there were some eggs right there on the ground for the easy grabs. I scanned the hedges and flower beds for flecks of colored shell.

"I want you older kids to stay where you are," he said. "I'm going to give the youngest ones a three-minute head start. After that, y'all will get twenty minutes to find your eggs."

He held the stop watch and lifted the bullhorn to his mouth. "GO!"

The women helped the youngest children pick up the obvious eggs. After a few minutes, Mr. Johnson signaled for us to start. The grounds suddenly became a flurry of bodies darting here and there. Kids were in trees and jammed into brushes. I caught Father and the sisters off the side pointing and laughing. I ran across the grass and dove under the nearby hedges. I scooped up a few eggs then ran toward some flower beds. Frances was hot on my heels. We exploded through the flowers and ferreted in between the stalks.

"Got one." She held up a plastic egg.

I didn't wait to see what she found inside, but took off to find more eggs. After the twenty minutes were up, Mr. Johnson raised his bullhorn and called all of us over to him.

"Okay, let's see what everyone's got," he said.

We all counted out eggs. Elaine Lugo had the most eggs, and Vivian found the golden egg. Inside Frances' plastic egg was a silver ring with a pretty blue stone. After Mr. Johnson handed out prizes—chocolate rabbits in varying sizes—he started making up prizes.

"Next prize goes to whichever hunter is wearing a dress."

We all giggled because all the girls had worn dresses.

"Now, the next prize goes to all those boys wearing shoes."

We all giggled again, and the boys claimed their prizes.

Everyone walked away with a chocolate rabbit and our egg-filled Easter baskets. We followed Father and the sisters to the cars and piled in. I got into Father's car.

"We're not going straight home," Father said. "We have a treat for you girls."

He and the sisters pulled out of the parking lot and drove a few minutes across town to a concert hall. He parked the car and we got out and gather all together in the parking lot.

"We have tickets for you all to see Mary Wells of Motown in concert," he said.

We entered the concert hall and were seated in the balcony section. I ran my fingers across the velvety chair seat and arms. When the curtains parted, she sauntered out onto stage in a long shiny silver dress and heels. Curly dollops of hair were piled high on her head. She was so glamorous. She nodded to the band and they started. When she started to sing, goosebumps chilled my arms.

After the concert, we entered the orphanage and could smell Aunt Rose working her magic. She went all out for Easter dinner. While we played in the playroom, we could hear the pots and lids clang and clash in the kitchen like a culinary symphony. The sisters whirred like drone bees around Aunt Rose as they sautéed, poured, whisked, and baked. The air in the house thickened sweet and salty, and warmth misted the windows.

By late afternoon, I could hardly stand my belly growls. We girls were finally led to the dining room where tables had been gussied up in fine linen, china plates, and candle light. Deviled eggs huddled on trays. The sisters poured us sweet iced tea, and then disappeared into the kitchen. They soon processed out carrying a feast—a silver platter with a brown sugar drizzled ham, bowls of greasy rice, sweet potato and pecan casserole, turnip greens cooked in pork fat, and fluffy buttermilk biscuits. My mouth went all tingly as water glands kicked into high gear. Father stood at the end of a long table, carved the ham and passed the plates down the table as though it was the Grinch's Roast Beast. Just when I thought I couldn't stuff in another bite, Aunt Rose appeared with Creole bread pudding with meringue. The food was so different from anything I had ever tasted, and it was nothing short of ambrosia.

A new girl came to live at the orphanage that spring. Her name was Bertha Richardson, and she looked to be about my age. She wasn't what you would call a pretty girl, because her face was mismatched. She had very small eyes that seemed way too little for her head. But she had very large lips which resembled two small eggplants. Now, having full lips and large expressive eyes would have made her look strikingly beautiful. Likewise, if she had small eyes and a tiny, delicate mouth, that would have given her a demure, elegant look. As it was, the top half of her face seemed to disagree with her bottom half.

Bertha was placed in the orphanage, but like many other girls there, she was not an orphan. In the beginning, she would disappear for days at a time, then reappear. Each time her family dropped her back off,

Bertha was moody and hostile, so we steered clear. Whatever her family situation was, I could only imagine it wasn't good.

One afternoon while playing in the back yard, I watched Bertha push a small girl off a swing and take the seat. The small girl brushed herself off and walked away. I knew it wasn't my business, but I couldn't look away. Bertha must have felt my stare, because she suddenly flicked her eyes at me and smiled—daring me to challenge her. We measured each other for a moment. Then, as though I wasn't even there, she broke the stare, pushed her feet against the ground, leaned back, and studied the clouds as the swing sailed back and forth.

That spring, Mother Clement Marie chose me to crown the Virgin in the May Crowning ceremony. A May Crowning is a traditional devotion in which a statue of the Blessed Virgin Mary is crowned in order to honor her as Queen of Heaven, Queen of Earth, and Queen of Peace. Usually, the Crowning takes place during a Mass devoted to Mary. At one point during the liturgy, a group of young girls dressed in white surrounds the statue of the Virgin. Then one of the girls, usually the youngest, places a wreath of fresh flowers on the statue's head.

The May Crowning is a big deal in Cuba. There, the most venerated and idolized image of the Virgin is known as *La Virgen de la Caridad* or the Virgin of Charity at *Cobre*. Legend has it that in the beginning of the 16th century, Spanish missionaries traveled to Cuba to convert the indigenous people to Catholicism. Around 1612, three boys, all named Juan, were caught in a terrible storm while fishing. The Virgin appeared to them on the tips of the waves holding the baby Jesus in her arms. Although the storm raged around them, she remained dry. She stood on a wooden plank with an inscription that read "I am the Virgin of Charity."

The statue of the Virgin of Charity was carved in Toledo, Spain so that their sailors could pray to her to protect them from pirates and storms at sea. The ship carrying the statue to Cuba from Spain smashed onto a coral reef in the Caribbean, but the statue somehow safely floated to Cuba. Several times the church tried to return the statue to Spain, and yet each time, something unexpected happened, and she returned home to Cuba. They finally took it as a sign that she wanted to stay, which explains why we feel such an attachment to her. We Cubans lovingly refer to her as "*Cachita*." Ernest Hemingway won the Nobel Prize in literature for *The Old Man and the Sea*. Afterward, he dedicated his medal to Cachita to honor both her and the country he loved.[35] Years later when people started to flee Cuba for Florida in rafts, people prayed to *La Virgen de la Caridad* for safe travels on the sea. You often see her image with the baby Jesus in her arms floating above three men, the three Juans, in a boat on a rough sea.

That spring, the May Crowning was to take place at Xavier University in New Orleans, one of the Catholic Universities there. They needed a little girl to crown the Virgin during the ceremony, so they asked Mother Clement Marie if she could select a young girl from our orphanage for them, and she volunteered me. I found out later that Bertha had really wanted to do it, but Mother insisted that I was to crown the Virgin.

The day arrived, and Paulette came to my bedroom, braided my hair and helped me into my pretty white dress. As I came down the stairs, Mother Clement Marie stood at the bottom of the stairs with a wreath of fresh white hawthorn blossoms in her hand. Hawthorn is considered sacred. Many historians believe that the Crown of Thorns worn by Jesus during his Crucifixion was made of hawthorn. She handed me the wreath.

"You look beautiful," she said.

"Thank you. I'm a little nervous."

"Don't be. You'll be fine."

She gripped her crutches and shuffled toward the door. We all piled into several cars and headed for the university. Once we entered the chapel and were seated in the front pews with the students, faculty and other priests and sisters seated behind us, the priest who was to celebrate the mass processed in with altar boys in tow. After communion, a soloist walked over to the microphone, and the priest nodded to me. I stood with the wreath in my hands and walked over to the statue of the Virgin just to the side of the altar. There was a ladder propped beside the statue. Father Coffey stood at the bottom of the ladder.

"I gotcha," he whispered.

As the soloist started to sing *On This Day, Oh Beautiful Mother*, I handed Father the wreath and climbed the ladder. I reached the top rung and leaned down to take the wreath. I turned back to the statue, and just as I reached out to place the wreath around the Virgin's head, I heard a loud crack. Somehow the top rung of the ladder broke. I lost my balance and pinwheeled backwards, and the wreath went flying. Luckily, Father was right there to catch me. I stepped down onto the second rung and steadied myself. Father retrieved the wreath from the floor and handed it to me. Half of the blossoms had been knocked off the side that hit the floor. With shaky hands, I positioned the part of the wreath with most of the surviving flowers toward the front of the statue. As I climbed down the ladder, I glanced out at the congregation. Bertha was beaming. Of course, there's no way she could have had anything to do with the ladder rung breaking, but my humiliation made her very happy.

Chapter NINETEEN

> *"Whenever I hear anyone arguing for slavery,*
> *I feel a strong impulse to see it tried on him personally."*
> — Abraham Lincoln

The Emancipation Proclamation was a presidential proclamation and executive order issued by President Abraham Lincoln on January 1, 1863 abolishing slavery for more than 3 million people. Although blacks in the South were no longer slaves, they weren't quite free. The Civil Rights Movement inspired many people to meet and march peacefully for a cause they believed in. Some protested willingly. Others were simply innocent bystanders of an oppressive, racist culture that was prepared to defend white supremacy at any cost. In many cases, both the willing protestor and the innocent bystander found themselves hosed, beaten, imprisoned, or murdered.

It wasn't just adults. There were many instances where children my age fell victim to racial hatred. In August 1955, while visiting his family in Money, Mississippi from Chicago, a 14-year-old boy named Emmett Till bought bubble gum in a store and was accused of flirting with a white female clerk. Her name was Carolyn Bryant and she just so happened to be the wife of the store's owner. According to Mrs. Bryant, she found herself alone in the store with Emmett who grabbed her wrist and asked for a date. Four days later, two men, the woman's husband Roy and his half-brother, J.W. Milam, dragged Emmett from his bed in the middle of the night and threw him in the back of a pickup truck. They drove to Milam's farm and took Till to the barn and pistol whipped him. They then drove to the Tallahatchie River and made Emmett carry a 75-pound cotton-gin fan out to the bank. They then ordered him to take off his clothes. The two men beat him nearly to death, gouged out his eye, shot him in the head, then fastened the cotton-gin fan to his neck with barbed wire before tossing him into the river. His remains were found three days later. Till's mother ordered that his casket remain open just so everyone can see what was done to poor Emmett.[36] After deliberating for only 67 minutes, the all-male, all-white jury acquitted the two men. Laughter broke out in the courtroom as the verdict was read. One juror later said that: "We wouldn't have taken so long if we hadn't stopped to drink pop."[37] After six decades, Carolyn Bryant finally admitted that she lied about what Emmett Till had done—that he had never grabbed her, harassed her, or asked her out.[38]

On Thursday, May 2, 1963, an estimated 1,500 children ranging from ages six to eighteen left their classrooms and gathered at the 16th Street Baptist Church in Birmingham, Alabama. From there they spilled out into the streets to peacefully march for civil rights in what was later dubbed the Birmingham Campaign or The Children's Crusade. Waiting police arrested them for parading without a permit, but the wave of kids kept coming. When the paddy wagons filled, they had to get a school bus to take the rest of them away. And yet, the kids kept coming. The next day, the children returned. The police were waiting for them with attack dogs. Even though the children were spat upon, bitten, beaten, and were bleeding, they continued to march peacefully. Frustrated, the police ordered the fire department to shoot high-pressure water hoses at the children, knocking them down and pinning them to park trees and to building walls. They screamed as the water tore at their clothing and flesh. And yet, they continued to march. For days. And they sang *Ain't Gonna Let Nobody Turn Me Around*. The news images of the brutality against those children shocked the world.[39] Whites, who until then had been afraid to support the Civil Rights Movement, watched the news feeds of those children singing the same songs they sang in church. They witnessed the bravery those children shone while marching despite the attack dogs and fire hoses. Seeing those images shifted people's reserve. Many whites joined the cause, and laws were changed.

During the time of slavery, New Orleans had the reputation of being the ultimate place of oppression. In the novel *Adventures of Huckleberry Finn* by Mark Twain, the runaway Jim takes off when he hears of a plan to "sell me down to Orleans" as though he was going to be sent to hell. So, it's interesting that after emancipation, the city played a central part in fighting for liberty and equality for all. It was by no means perfect, but the New Orleans that I saw in the early 1960s challenged Jim Crow laws: black children attended the white schools; blacks boycotted white stores in organized shop outs; blacks sued universities for admittance; black and white members of CORE (Congress of Racial Equality) staged peaceful sit-ins at the Woolworth's counter. Blacks in the South were making strides in the fight for Civil Rights, but there were many setbacks, too.

The Birmingham Campaign had been so successful, on May 10, 1963, many public facilities like lunch counters, drinking fountains, and fitting rooms became desegregated. At that time, Birmingham was one of the most notoriously racist cities in the South and home to one of the most violent chapters of the Ku Klux Klan. White who were still opposed to any kind of mixing with blacks began a campaign of their own. They set off homemade bombs in churches and homes all across the city. The bombings were so frequent the city acquired the nickname "Bombingham."

On Sunday morning, September 15th, four months after The Children's Crusade, a white man was seen stashing a box under the front steps of the 16th Street Baptist Church. Parishioners were getting ready for the 11 a.m. service. Five girls were in the basement putting on their choir robes. At 10:22 a.m., the box under the front steps which contained 19 sticks of dynamite exploded. Cynthia Wesley, Carole Robertson and Addie Mae Collins, all 14, and Denise McNair, 11 were found dead beneath the rubble in a basement restroom. Ten-year-old Sarah Collins was also in the restroom at the time of the explosion. She survived, but lost her right eye. More than 20 other people were injured in the blast.

Four members of a KKK splinter group, Robert E. Chambliss who was known as "Dynamite Bob," Bobby Frank Cherry, Herman Frank Cash, and Thomas E. Blanton, were suspected. The local authorities had no interest in solving the crime let alone charging anyone. Even though the FBI took over the investigation, their interest in the case was lukewarm at best.[40]

In October 1963, Chambliss was eventually arrested and charged with murder and possession of dynamite without a permit. On October 8, 1963, Chambliss was found not guilty in state court of murder. He was sentenced to six months in jail for possessing dynamite without a permit and fined $100.[41]

After the trial, a Klan member said that he and many good, God-fearing, like-minded Christians thought that Negroes' lives were as significant as a tick or a flea. A tick or a flea. When you hear things like that, those sick words infect your being. They seep way down deep into your tissue and bone where they sit and fester like a cancerous mass.

It's truly terrible for parents to teach their children to hate. It's just as terrible for a child to learn that some people will hate you simply for existing. The world doesn't have to be the way the world is. Good people can act, and the world can be better, and so can we. Time has a way of mending that fear and distrust. You meet wonderful people who treat you with kindness and decency. But then the Trayvon Martins, Michael Browns, Eric Garners and Emanuel African Methodist Episcopal Churches happen, and there you are again in that dark place, and you find that that cancerous mass has suddenly flared, and just like that, you're out of remission.

Let me clarify—I know not all white people are racist. In fact, I believe in my heart that by far, most everyone is good and decent and not racist at all. That said, I have heard and read angry assertions by some racist white people that claim we blacks (and Latinos) are taking over the country. I find that ironic given the fact that long before the African

Americans' black ancestors were yanked from their homes and pitched naked and terrified onto crowded cargo ships to labor in plantations across the South, their white ancestors were the ones who had invaded this country and stole the land from the Native Americans. Yet, you don't see them tomahawking the hell out of the palefaces, now do you?

Chapter TWENTY

That fall, Bertha attended school with me and Frances, but she seemed indifferent to her studies. She passed the time in class doodling in the margins of her notebook and slipping girls notes when the sisters weren't looking. I wanted to do well in school, so I studied hard, finished my homework on time, and answered questions in class. One day as I raised my hand, I heard Bertha in the back of the room mutter "suck up" under her breath, and the girls snickered.

One evening not long after, I walked through the playroom and saw Bertha sitting alone in the corner playing jacks.

"Are you done with your homework?" I asked.

"Done enough."

"Don't let Sister Paulette hear you say that."

"I just don't see the point. What good is math and science to a housemaid."

"You don't have to be a housemaid. You can be whatever you set your mind to."

She just shook her head, bounced the ball, and swiped up the jacks.

Another rainy afternoon, I noticed Bertha sitting alone again in the playroom. She looked as though she had been crying. She had visited her family earlier that day. I had heard a rumor that her mother would discipline her by thrusting Bertha's body up onto a red-hot stove and burning her. I understood why Bertha was so mean. Her anger was like a covered pot that had been left too long on the stove. A slight bump of the lid sent the steam pouring out. That day, she looked so lonely and dejected that I felt sorry for her. I walked over and sat beside her.

"You want to play checkers?" I asked.

She shrugged, but didn't say no, so I got out the board and set up the pieces. At one point in the game, my piece reached the opposite side of the board.

"King me," I said.

"No."

"What do you mean no? You have to king me. That's the rule."

"What do you know? You think you're better than everyone else, but I know that you're nothing but a stupid saltwater nigger."

I wanted to say something back, but I was so shocked that I couldn't speak. An I'm-just-joking smile slowly bloomed. I started to smile back, but she drew back her hand and slapped me across the face.

"No one tells me what to do."

I brushed the pieces off the board onto the playroom floor and stood.

"You better watch your back," I heard her say under her breath as I walked out the door.

The next morning while Paulette braided my hair, I told her what had happened.

"It sounds like she has it out for you," Paulette said.

"Why? I haven't done anything to her."

"That doesn't matter. Someone who is wounded looks to lash out at someone with a weak spot. That's how they can feel they have power and control."

"I don't have any weak spots."

"Maybe not. I'd still watch my back if I were you."

Our teacher that year was Sister Enda. She was a plump woman with a soft, kind voice. On our first day of class, Sister had a bad case of the hiccups, so from then on, behind her back we referred to her as Sister Hiccup.

As usual, Sister Hiccup entered the classroom and asked us to pass our homework forward. I opened my backpack, but my homework wasn't there. My heart started to race. I took my books out and shook them, but no homework. It simply wasn't there.

"Catalina, what are you doing?" Sister Hiccup asked.

"I'm looking for my homework. I finished it and put it in my bag, but it's not here."

She let out a sigh. "I didn't expect this from you. I'm very disappointed."

Sister shook her head as she turned her attention to the blackboard and began her lessons. I glanced over at Bertha in the next row, who was smiling. I wanted to do well in school more than anything, and she knew it. Bertha had found my weak spot. After that day, I hid my homework under my pillow at night. In the morning, I folded the papers into a tight square and tucked them into a pocket as soon as I dressed, then stashed them in my book bag just before leaving for school.

That fall, St. Augustine held a talent show. Father Coffey taught English at the all-boys school, and he volunteered us girls to participate. There were fifteen events scheduled, and he asked me, Juana, Frances, Maria, and Vivian to dance a traditional Cuban dance. We decided to dance the mambo which is an eight-beat dance where you step on the second and sixth beats. Quick quick slow, quick quick slow. With your arms up and out at your side, you shake your hips and twist your torso letting your body sway to the beat. The five of us practiced our steps in the playroom after school.

As I mentioned, we girls were expected to do the household chores, and each month we rotated our duties. That month, Bertha worked in the sewing room with Sister Paulette making our costumes for the show. The week before the show, Sister called us Cuban girls into the sewing room.

"I have a surprise for you." She poured colorful fabric onto the sewing table from a shopping bag. "Bertha's grandmother is a longtime friend of mine. When she heard about the talent show, she wanted to help in some way. She went to the library and found a book on Cuba. She saw traditional dance costumes in the book and made these skirts for you."

Sister held one of them up to Vivian's waist. It was a flowing white skirt with bold stripes of red and blue made from a light cotton material.

They were the colors of the Cuban flag. There was a red sash around the waist and ruffles around the bottom hem. It was beautiful.

"We just need to tailor them for each of you," Bertha said.

We all stepped into a skirt, and Sister gathered and pinned the material at our waists and at our knees.

"We should have these finished in a day or two," Sister said.

"This show is going to be great," Frances said.

Sister sat behind the sewing machine and started to mend one of the skirts. "It will be memorable."

The night of the show, all of the acts gathered backstage and in the wings waiting their turn to go on. Sister Paulette and Bertha touched up our makeup and made adjustments to our skirts. Father directed groups on and off the stage. When it was just about time for us to go on, he waved to us and positioned us in the wings.

"You girls are up next. You look fabulous. Are you ready?"

We held hands and nodded.

"I'm nervous," Maria whispered.

"Don't be," Father whispered back. "You'll knock them out. Now, go break a leg."

Break a leg? Why on earth would he say such a horrible thing? I thought I may have misunderstood him, but I didn't get the chance to ask. The announcer called our names, and Father nudged us onto the stage. We positioned ourselves in an arc and waited for the music to begin. The spotlights were warm and bright. I could hear people shifting in the audience, but I couldn't see anyone's faces. My heart pounded against my ribs so wildly that I thought for sure they all could hear it.

The minute I heard the familiar music begin, the music from my home, I let out a sigh. I closed my eyes and imagined how a bird must feel when it has flown far from its nest, and it hears a familiar song from its homeland. I listened to the rhythm of the music and let myself go. I thought about Mima and how she loved to play the radio, how Pipo loved to sing and dance, and all the times when Nené taught me these dance steps in our living room. The memories of my family and my home flooded my mind.

We began to dance, stepping backwards and forwards. The arc swept back and forth across the stage, then morphed into a circle, then back into an arc. I heard the rhythmic clapping of the audience, and my spirit soared. The five of us swayed in perfect harmony. At one point, I caught Frances' eye, and we laughed. I was having the time of my life, and I felt proud to be Cuban.

Just then I felt something give. As I shook my hips, the stitches in my skirt suddenly started to unravel. I quickly lowered my arms to secure my skirt, but it was too late. It had slipped below my waist and had twisted around my thighs. The more I tugged at the fabric, the more the stitches unraveled. I ran off the stage in my underwear gripping the rag that was once my pretty skirt. Behind me, I heard the audience howl with laughter.

As soon as I reached backstage, one of the sisters wrapped me in a towel. Father ran to my side of the backstage and hugged me. I buried my face into his jacket and sobbed. As soon as the dance finished, the girls rushed from the stage to my side.

"What happened to your skirt?" Maria asked.

I couldn't answer her. I pushed my face further into Father's jacket. The sister who had wrapped me in a towel took over for Father and directed the next group onto the stage. He knelt down beside me.

"I'm so sorry that happened to you," he said wiping my cheek with his handkerchief. "You might not be able to understand this now, but you have been blessed because you are being tested. Whoever God chooses to test comes out stronger in the end. Gold is tested by fire, and there can be no rainbow without light shimmering through the rain."

Vivian, Frances, Maria, and Juana huddled around me. Bertha and Sister Paulette were in the darkened wings on the other side of the stage, but I could see that they were pointing and laughing at me. I can never be sure if they had intentionally meant to sabotage my performance. But then again, my skirt was the only one to have come undone.

Chapter TWENTY-ONE

Karma circles both good and bad back around. Just before Christmas, one of Bertha's uncles came to the orphanage and took her away for good. I later heard that it was because her grandfather had committed suicide. I never understood the connection between her living at the orphanage and her grandfather's death, but we never saw her again. It was true that I didn't like Bertha. Still, I understood that she was so mean because she was so unhappy. I couldn't help feeling sorry for her. After all, no one is truly good or truly bad. Every saint hides a skeleton in the cupboard, and every villain has a mother who calls him Sonny.

I no longer had Bertha to torment me, and I felt as though I was riding high on a wave. Just when I thought my luck had changed for the better, the wave crashed back down. Right after the holidays, Mother Clement Marie was removed from our orphanage and forced to retire. Her health had been steadily dwindling, and although she could fulfill her duties, her debilitating arthritis made it nearly impossible for her to climb the stairs. She tried to hide it, but we all knew that she was in constant pain. Overnight, they moved her to a retirement home for sisters on the other side of town.

We were told that she would be leaving the night before, but we weren't allowed to speak with her. Instead, we laid in our beds and listened to the sisters down the hall laugh and cry as they helped her pack her things, which made me cry too. The next morning, I looked for Mother at mass, but she wasn't there. I was so afraid that I had missed her, but as soon as the final hymn was sung, we girls raced downstairs to see her standing by the front door. We flocked around her and sobbed.

She reached out to each one of us individually and held our faces in her palm. When the time came for her to say good bye to me, I was crying so hard I started to hiccup.

"My Catalina." she wiped a tear with her thumb. "You will be with your family one day soon. And you will do great things."

The pain in my heart was so intense that it rose up into my throat and sealed it tightly. I wanted to thank her, to say that I loved her, to tell her that I would never forget her kindness, but nothing came out. She smiled and moved on to the next girl.

After she had said her personal goodbyes to everyone, Father opened the door and carried her bags onto the front porch. She turned toward the door to leave, but looked back one last time. It was clear that she didn't want to go, but her pain and religious politics gave her no choice.

That afternoon after I had finished my chores, I went to my bedroom to be alone instead of joining the girls outside. I had been crying all morning and was exhausted. I missed Mother as much as I had missed my own family. In some ways, she was more of a mother figure to me than Mima ever was. I laid on my bed and stared at the smoldering clouds above the tree tops that had turned the sky black velvet. I knew I would never forget her or the love she showed me. Now, many years later, what I remember and admire most about her was her ability to love people with their flaws. The sisters were flawed. Father, flawed. Me, certainly flawed. And yet, she loved us anyway, despite, and maybe even because of our flaws.

Was it luck or providence that brought me to that particular orphanage? Some say there are no coincidences in life, and that everything is predestined. Was it indeed luck? Perhaps. That reminded me of a story I once heard about a wise Indian chief. One day, a beautiful wild stallion entered their village. The elders all remarked that that was a lucky sign.

"Perhaps," the chief replied.

The following day, the stallion ran away. The elders agreed that that was very unlucky.

"Perhaps," the chief said.

When the chief's son went out into the fields with a group of boys his own age, they found the stallion grazing on prairie grass. It wandered over to the son, and he gently led it back to the village.

"How lucky you are for your son to have such a beautiful horse," the elders exclaimed.

"Perhaps," the chief said.

The following day, his son tried to ride the stallion, and it bucked him off, breaking the boy's arm.

"How unlucky for your son," the elders said.

Again, the chief said, "Perhaps."

Later that week, a neighboring tribe waged war on their tribe. All the young men left the village to fight, but because the chief's son had broken his arm, he stayed behind and didn't fight. And his life was spared.

Was it luck or providence that led me to that orphanage and brought Mother Clement Marie into my life? In my heart, I think it was a little of both.

The following day, we got a new Mother Superior. Her name was Mother Ann Marie, and she was Sister Paulette's younger sibling. Mother Ann Marie was in her early 30s and had the same light skin and Asian eyes as Sister Paulette. Her movements were very feminine, almost sensual. She ambled through the halls as a majestic deer might stroll across a meadow. She had a voluptuous body and knew how to wield her beauty in order to turn heads in any room. A black Marilyn Monroe, there wasn't a mirror she passed up without adjusting her habit or inspecting her lipstick. I remembering thinking her looks were anything but plain and her behavior was anything but humble and sisterly. Nevertheless, it was pretty clear she thought the sun came up just to hear her crow.

Mother Ann Marie wasn't mean like Sister Paulette. She was simply indifferent and ineffective. She addressed us girls with disinterest in weak, monotone sentences that sometimes seemed as though she had been partially drained of her blood. I suppose the adults caught on to her apathy and silly behavior, because after nine months she was suddenly transferred to another assignment. Sister Paulette never told us the reason why she was sent away, and we never asked.

The next Mother Superior to be assigned to us was named Mother Marie Fidelis. Fidelis! Oh, my God, of all names for a Cuban to have to bear! She had very dark skin and a tall, broad frame with a face that life had chewed on. If a roughed up black man had dressed up as nun for Halloween, he would look like Mother Fidelis. She had big feet, and her thick, dark eyebrows furrowed downward like the outstretched wings of a crow. She was a black Cruella De Vil.

The following afternoon, we changed out of our school clothes, and because it was raining, instead of heading out to the back yard, we made a beeline to the playroom to watch TV. It was gone. The TV stand was still there, but a piece of Plexiglass had been place on top of the stand, and underneath it was a piece of paper. I lifted a corner of the glass and slid the paper out.

"What is it?" Maria asked.

It was a handwritten list. Whoever had written it must have been pretty mad, because the thick black ink seemed to have been gouged onto the paper.

"It's a list of reasons why Mother Fidelis doesn't want us to watch TV."

We played outside most nice weather days and had books and games to entertain us, but there was something special about gathering together to watch TV afterschool. On movie nights with the sisters and Father, Aunt Rose popped us bowls of popcorn, and we flopped like ragdolls all over the chairs, sofa, and floor. The girls gathered around me as I read.

1. Watching television corrupts the mind.
2. Watching television is time away from prayer and reflection.
3. Watching television ruins eyesight.
4. Watching television keeps girls from doing God's work.
5. Watching television takes time away from homework.
6. Watching television teaches promiscuity and lewdness in young girls.

7. Watching television encourages women's independence and free thinking.
8. Watching television will lead to the downfall of proper society.
9. Girls must be quiet and obey.
10. Mother Fidelis forbids the watching of television. Period.

Living in Cuba, I had reached my limit of accepting the machismo attitude where women mustn't think for themselves, but do what men said because they knew better. Don't get me wrong, I don't disrespect authority. But that day, when I read that we girls were to be quiet and obey, that got my hackles up.

"What kind of nonsense is this?" I said. "Girls must be quiet and obey. Says who?"

"Says me."

We all spun around to see Mother Fidelis hovering in the doorway. Her voice was loud and honking and carried throughout the halls. She had a thick wooden dust brush in her hand. She slapped her palm with it slowly as she approached us. As it became apparent she was closing in on me, the rest of the girls parted like the Red Sea. She stopped in front of me and leaned down.

"I had a feeling you might be the ring leader."

She drew her arm back and struck me with the brush. I'm not sure exactly where it landed, because the pain exploded all over my body. I hit the floor and saw stars. I tried to get up, but the room swirled, so I laid back down. Mother Fidelis slithered up beside me and towered over me.

"Girls must be quiet and obey. Is that understood."

Although she addressed all the girls, her eyes never left me.

"Let this be a lesson to anyone who tries to challenge me. Now, get up."

I pushed myself up onto an elbow. Maria stepped forward to help me, but was blocked by Mother Fidelis's brush.

"She can do it."

I wobbled to my feet and stood still. She positioned herself right in front of me, but I didn't move. We stood nose to nose in a staring contest like a drill sergeant breaking a new recruit in boot camp. I held her stare. I was also holding my pee, but I didn't want her to know that. She finally broke her gaze.

"Catalina, meet me in the infirmary now," she said over her shoulder as she left the room.

I followed her upstairs and into the infirmary.

"Sit down."

I sat on a bed and waited, but she said nothing. Instead, she walked back out the door closing it behind her. The lock clanked.

"You'll stay in here until you learn to behave. I won't stand for insurrection."

With that, I watched the shadow from her big feet under the door disappear. Later that night, Mother Fidelis unlocked the door and Frances came in carrying my supper on a tray. She kept her eyes on the floor and placed the tray on the night stand.

"You can go now, Frances."

Frances scurried out of the room. Mother Fidelis lifted the top slice of bread on the sandwich on my tray and inspected what was inside.

"It seems to me you might need a little encouragement in learning this lesson. I'll let the teacher know you won't be in school for a few days."

"What? You can't do that. I have an exam."

She replaced the slice of bread with a sigh. "Well, you'll just have to make that up."

Until that point, I had been angry. After that moment, I was afraid. How much power did she have if the rest of the sisters and Father were okay with her keeping me locked in there?

After four days, she let me out. I don't know what Mother Fidelis told the other girls about me, but I was a pariah. They steered clear of me, and for my own survival, I steered clear of Mother Fidelis.

One afternoon while on kitchen duty, Mother Fidelis came in to get a snack from the refrigerator. I stood at the stove and kept my eyes on the purple blue pilot light flame. I heard the suck of the refrigerator door open. I glanced over my shoulder and watched her stare with indecision at the food. I decided then and there to break the ice.

"Is there anything I can get you?" I asked.

She faced me and raised an eyebrow. I reached for a plate on the counter.

"I made these cookies. Would you like one?"

I held the plate of cookies out to her. She puckered her lips and examined the tray as though it held a tangle of snakes.

"Chocolate chip. I heard they were your favorite."

She lifted one from the plate with her pinky extended.

"Thank you, Catalina."

"You're welcome, Grandmama."

I have no idea what possessed me to call her that, but it had the desired effect. She cocked her head, and a smile crooked one side of her face. As she left the kitchen, it was clear that she thought she had defeated me. I never felt that way, though, because to defeat someone is to take something from them. Instead, I thought of it as my way of managing her.

Chapter TWENTY-TWO

Black students in the South had had enough. They were tired of waiting for politicians and pastors to do something about segregation, so they took matters into their own hands, and a peaceful movement was born. On February 1, 1960, in Greensboro, NC, four black men from North Carolina Agricultural and Technical State University sat down at the Woolworth's whites only counter and ordered donuts and coffee. Ezell Blair Jr., David Richmond, Franklin McCain, and Joseph McNeil were refused service. Though they expected to get arrested, nothing happened. They remained at the counter doing their homework until closing time. By February 5th, three hundred students joined them at the counter.[42]

Soon, similar peaceful sit-ins were staged all over the South. On Friday, September 9, 1960, seven students, five black and two white, organized the first lunch counter sit-in in New Orleans. The students were members of the Congress on Racial Equality or CORE. At 10:30 a.m., they arrived at the Woolworth's near the French Quarter on the corner of Canal and N. Rampart and took their seats at the counter. Six police officers were called to the scene in case there was any trouble, but they never tried to remove the students. After they were refused service, they politely announced that they intended to remain at the counter. The white customers remained there as well and continued to be served while the students sat calmly smoking and chatting with one another.[43] At 12:30 p.m., two hours after the sit-in began, the owner closed the counter.

Years later, by 1964, it was still illegal for blacks to dine in a public restaurant. Some establishments would allow black customers to buy take out. It was understood that while they waited for their food, black patrons had to stand up straight and keep their eyes forward as their order was filled. They couldn't slouch or look around, because if they showed poor posture or glanced at a white patron seated at the counter, they could have been considered threatening. Ironically, many of the wait staff were black, but weren't permitted to sit down and enjoy a meal. I remember seeing Bible verses tacked to the wall behind a lunch counter, yet I'm sure the restaurant owner believed in his heart that what he was doing, or not doing, was Christian. As soon as the black customer's order was up, the waitress handed them the to-go bag, and they promptly left.

On July 2, 1964, the Civil Rights Act was signed into law by President Lyndon B. Johnson. Many restaurant owners throughout the South feared that they would have trouble sitting blacks and whites next to each other. Some owners sued the federal government saying they had no right to come in and tell them what to do with their businesses. Southern politicians argued that it was their states' right to defend segregation claiming that their religion commanded that blacks and whites eat separately. Oh, but it was perfectly fine to take a black person's money, just as long as they didn't have to watch them eat.

The U.S. Supreme Court ruled unanimously against the restaurant owners. Southern politicians were in a rage over the decision, but the court held fast declaring that Congress may determine what goes on at the state level if it effects interstate commerce.[44]

I remember walking the aisles of the Woolworth's and occasionally glancing toward the dining section at the white patrons seated at the counter. I had never eaten in a restaurant in Cuba or the United States. Although seeing those white folks enjoying their white bread sandwiches and banana splits stung, I would no sooner think to go over there and sit down than to swim across the ocean.

Shortly after the Civil Rights Act had passed, Mother Fidelis decided to test drive the new law. One afternoon after school, she strode across the back yard toward me. She pointed to Frances, Maria and Vivian and waved to them to sit next to me in the grass.

"Tomorrow afternoon, you four will go to Woolworth's and enjoy dessert."

We all sat there with our mouth open, staring at her like statutes.

"Will that be dangerous?" Vivian finally asked.

"Nonsense. President Johnson declared that blacks and whites can eat together. The whites don't care that you're Cuban and not African American. They only see black faces."

"Will you take us," Maria asked.

"No. A very nice white couple I know will pick you up tomorrow, eat with you, and bring you back home. It's settled."

She turned on her heels and disappeared inside.

The following afternoon, Mother asked us to follow her to the clothes rack. She swooped back in forth in front of the rack choosing our outfits.

"Now, you don't want to appear too fancy," she said flipping hangers. "You don't want to call too much attention to yourselves." She pulled hangers off the rack and handed them to us. "At the same time, you want to look like fine, respectable young ladies."

Mother held out a pair of navy blue shorts, a white and blue cotton top and nice white shoes for me. After we dressed and had our hair done in the beauty parlor out back, we were instructed to sit in the front parlor and wait for the white couple. When they came to the front door, Mother greeted them.

"Girls, this is Mr. and Mrs. Slater."

They stepped into the parlor and shook our hands. Both the Slaters were tall and thin with dark hair and friendly smiles.

"We're going to have fun," Mrs. Slater said.

They headed toward the front door and motioned for us to follow them. We drove about 10 minutes to the same Woolworth's near the French Quarter made famous by the 1960 CORE sit-in. The couple parked the car on the street, and we followed them inside. We all sat down together in a booth, and the waitress and owner walked toward our booth to take our order. The waitress was a black girl in her late teens. She had shoulder length straightened hair and bangs that swept off to one side of her face like soft black bird feathers. She wore a white, short-sleeved uniform dress that had a red and white checkered apron and the same checkered piping around the collar and sleeves. She cautiously approached our booth as though there might have been snakes on the table. The owner stood beside her and nodded to her. She looked at him then back at us and swallowed hard.

"It's okay," he said to her. "You can take their order just like everyone else."

She let out a shaky sigh and went around the table asking each of us what we wanted. When it was my turn, she smiled at me and waited, pencil hovering above her pad.

"May I have a root beer float, please?"

"Sure."

"But can I have chocolate ice cream instead of vanilla?"

"Of course."

The desserts came and we talked to the Slaters about school and music and the movies. I don't remember the people around us making any fuss. I had no idea that what we had just done was such a huge deal. The significance was completely lost on me. There could have been photographers or the press or TV cameras, but I was blissfully unaware. That might have been a good thing. I might have been too nervous to enjoy my float. I'm afraid if a reporter had asked me my thoughts on what was happening, I might have said something like, "I don't know about you guys, but I'm all about this ice cream."

I do remember that when we were finished, the owner came over to our table. We all thanked him for the delicious treats.

"It's my pleasure," he said. "I want you girls to know that no one can ever keep you from eating here ever again. Y'all, please come back anytime."

Mr. Slater paid the bill, and we followed him and Mrs. Slater outside, climbed back into the car and drove home. Unlike so many violent clashes over integration before, during and after our trip to Woolworth's that day, ours was a quiet, peaceful triumph. You might say it was a training session for both sides.

Chapter **TWENTY-THREE**

Before we left Cuba, my brother, Lazaro, had been given a 30-year sentence for becoming a counterrevolutionary, but in the fall of 1964, he was released from prison. Although Pete told me and Mario that amazing great news in a letter, he never mentioned the details. Many years later, I asked Lazaro why he had been given clemency, but he only shook his head and waved me off. It was never spoken of in our family, but we all thought that someone had waved a magic wand and said "Your papers have been straightened out, so you can go now." I have a feeling none of us will ever know the truth. Not that it matters. I was happy for him and his wife, Victoria, but I couldn't help fearing that the government would realize their mistake, and the decision would somehow, someday, be reversed.

School started up again that fall. I was eleven years old and in sixth grade. Two years had passed since I left Cuba. I rarely saw or spoke to Mario. Whenever we did visit, I found him bitter and aggressive. I received occasional letters from Pete, always with the promise of our family reuniting one day soon. I saw him just one afternoon a year, the week before Christmas.

Before we left Cuba, Nené had also promised me and Mario that we wouldn't be left alone in the United States for very long. I had begun to doubt him and Pete and was afraid that I might never see my family again. I had always known that doing well in school was my ticket to greater things, but I had found a new purpose. I thought if I could do well in school and get a good paying job, I could make enough money to gather my family together by myself. I had no idea how I was going to do that, but I knew I had to try.

I started to see the orphanage less like a pit stop and more like a home. Inside its protective walls, I felt safe. Outside, however, I felt the white folks' displeasure—in stores, on buses, and in the street. You were either invisible to them, or whenever you were noticed, looked down upon, sneered at, or openly humiliated. To be clear, I didn't experience that from every white person I met, of course. But the possibility of a bad encounter was a constant buzz in the background, so I never quite knew how to interact with white folks I didn't know. I didn't know who I could trust, so I felt I could never let my guard down. I was glad that I went to an all-black school. Maria and Vivian, because they were lighter-skinned, integrated the white schools. I was so dark-skinned, there was no way I could ever pull that off. There was no fitting me in, and that was fine by me.

A week after school started, Sister Paulette was suddenly transferred from our orphanage and given a new assignment. Apparently, Mother Fidelis had called her into her office out of the blue and broke the news. Within an hour, her bags were packed and she was gone. I confess I wasn't unhappy to see her go, but you could tell that her immediate departure made the rest of the sisters fearful as though the sword of Damocles dangled above each of them.

A few days later, yet another one of Sister Paulette's siblings, Sister Celeste, came to live with us. She was short and had a beautiful figure like Mother Ann Marie and the same Asian eyes as her sisters, but her skin was much lighter than the others. In fact, it was so light that if you saw her on the street, you would have sworn she was white. Unlike her siblings, she was a very pleasant woman. She took to her tasks with pleasure and walked the halls with a smile. She seemed like a woman without a care in the world. I'm sure she had her worries like everyone else, but she never let them show. She made life in the orphanage easier for all of us. I learned from her the power of a smile. It has the power to light up a room on the dullest of days. It immediately defuses tension.

Cousin to the warm hug, it is love's secret weapon—easy to carry and effortless to wield.

Fall faded to winter and before I knew it, Christmas was upon us once more. Pete had come to see Mario and me the first two Christmases, so naturally I expected to see him again. But in a letter he wrote two weeks before Christmas, he apologized for not being able to make it that year. I sat on my bed and reread it, feeling the unfair warmth from the paper instead of from Pete's hands. He seemed so far away from me. After carefully folding the letter and tucking it back into the envelope, I placed it into a box in the drawer beside my bed where I kept all his letters—an anchor to the past and lifeline to the future of an imagined life in which my house is filled with family and life is good. I sat on my bed and expected to feel devastated, but I wasn't. I felt indifferent to him not coming to see me. I was numbing myself in order to cope. Like a silent thief, time pulls people apart.

Christmas came with usual fanfare of decorations, silver trays brimming with twirls of colorful ribbon candies, spicy ginger bread, and iced sugar cookies, Motown concerts, and of course, a visit from Santa Claus. I still kept my distance, but began to admire the custom. I relished the lightness of the Christmas season. It was as though everyone had pressed the pause button on life's worries. People chatted openly to each other on the buses and in the streets, and well wishes flowed sweet as egg nog.

I savored the walks home from school that time of year. Dusk came earlier then, and

the evening flowed between the houses and paused on the front lawns in the glow of bayed windows. It had the quality of a honeyed memory. Frances, Maria, Vivian and I marveled from the sidewalk through gauzy curtains at the fancy decorations and lighted Christmas trees inside people's houses. I imagined family scenarios of those unknown, unseen people: the handsome father coming home from an easy day at the office; the beautiful mother readying the table for a delicious dinner; the intelligent children, having already finished their homework, regaling the family with the A on the chemistry exam or the winning volleyball spike in gym class; then after clearing the table and washing the dishes, the whole family gathering in the den in front of the fire to share their evening before climbing into their cozy beds. It was a silly game to play, I know, but it gave me a warm sense of home.

One morning after the New Year, Mother Fidelis suddenly appeared in the dining room doorway as we ate breakfast. She clapped her hands, and we fell silent, expecting the worst.

"You girls have behaved very well this Christmas season. As a reward, I want to give you a little money to get a sweet treat for yourselves at the Five and Dime on your way home from school. Be back by four."

Mother nodded once and was gone. The sisters passed out five pennies each for us. I dropped mine into the pocket of my dress.

The Five and Dime was a few blocks from the orphanage. As soon as school ended, Frances and I met up with Vivian and Maria. I felt a sudden surge of freedom and began to skip along the sidewalk. Once we entered the store, I noticed Paulette beside the glass cases filled with wrapped candies in every flavor you could imagine. We sidled up beside her and marveled at the vast selection as a man dying of thirst in the desert might gaze upon an oasis.

"I'm going to buy three watermelon and two cherry candies, please," Frances said.

The woman behind the counter smiled at us as we pointed to our choices. She scooped the candies into tiny paper bags. I decided on root beer, butterscotch, coconut, grape, and lime and handed my palm-warmed pennies to the woman. With cheeks jammed with sweet nuggets like squirrels stashing nuts, we wandered up and down the brightly colored aisles with their green and white checkered linoleum floors. Shelf after shelf overflowed with toys and hair combs and ballpoint pens. We rode up and down the escalators, pretending we were rich women in fur coats in a fancy department store. I spied the clock on the wall.

"We have to get back for dinner," I said.

"We still have time," Paulette said.

"But it's been an hour. Mother said to be back by four o'clock."

"Since when do you care about rules?"

"I don't want to get into trouble."

"You mean you don't want to feel that dust brush again," Paulette laughed.

Her teasing stung. "Neither would you, trust me."

Paulette considered this for a moment. "Okay, you win. We'll go. But first, let's walk pass the candies again. I think I'd like one or two for the road."

"But we don't have any more money," Maria said.

Paulette grinned and headed toward the candy aisle. "They won't miss a few pieces."

I pulled the back of her coat. "No, Paulette. You can't do that."

She stopped and turned. "Oh, yes I can. If you don't want to do it, then don't."

She spun on her heels and quickened her pace toward the candy aisle. She bellied up to the glass case and nodded a hello to the woman behind the counter. As soon as woman turned her back, Paulette snatched a handful of candies, tucked them into her coat pocket, and calmly walked out the door. I was so shocked I stood frozen in the aisle.

"Caty, let's go," Maria said.

I ran out of the store and down the street. We raced up the porch steps and through the front door. As we climbed the stairs and headed to our bedroom, Paulette nudged me, laughing.

"I told you I could do it."

We draped our coats on our beds and headed back downstairs.

Later that night, there came a knock on the front door, and Mother Fidelis answered. It was the owner of the Five and Dime. He still wore his white apron from the store. He removed his hat and scratched his bald head.

"Mr. Johnson, what a pleasure. Please come in. What can we do for you?"

"No thank you, Mother. I just thought you should know that one of your girls took some candy this afternoon without paying."

"What?"

She took a step back and peered into the playroom at us. Mr. Johnson stayed planted on the porch, but leaned inside around the doorpost. We all glared at Paulette, who kept her eyes focused on her Old Maid cards.

"I don't know exactly which girl took the candy," Mr. Johnson said, "but my counter girl saw one of your girls take some and put it into her coat pocket before leaving the store."

"Thank you for letting me know. I'm so sorry this happened, and I can assure you, this will never happen again. We've always had a good relationship with you and the store. I hope this hasn't broken your trust."

"No ma'am."

"I'll make sure the girls make this up to you."

Mother closed the door, then turned and went straight up the stairs.

"The coats!" Maria said.

Paulette's eyes widened.

We stumbled up the stairs and down the hall, but skidded to a stop just as Mother stepped out of our bedroom holding Paulette's coat.

"I don't care if only one of you took this candy. You will all go back tomorrow after school and apologize. Paulette, you will pay Mr. Johnson back for these candies."

"But I don't have any money."

"You should have thought of that before you committed the crime. You'll work off that money here in the orphanage under my supervision, then personally hand that money to Mr. Johnson. Now, all of you, to bed. Not you, Paulette. You will come with me."

Mother was so angry, she seemed to give off smoke. We crept past her with our eyes glued to the rug or the wallpaper. I could feel the blistering heat of her stare. Before I entered the bedroom, I glanced back at Paulette and caught her eye. We both knew that Mother was going to give her the dust brush. She was no longer laughing.

Chapter TWENTY-FOUR

That March, I turned twelve. I noticed that my body had curves that it hadn't had just a few months before. One morning as I stepped out of the shower, I passed a misted mirror and did a double take. I stood for a moment facing the glass with my towel wrapped and knotted above my breasts. I wiped the mist from the mirror with my palm in a large oval, then I opened the towel and gazed at my body. As steam circled my shoulders, I stared at myself as though I was a stranger. I had noticed that I had grown taller than most of the girls my age, but the face I saw staring back at me was more angular, less babyish. I had hair in places where I had been bare. I had recently gotten my period, and my breasts were rounder than they had ever been. I smiled at my reflection, rewrapped the towel, and headed toward the clothes rack.

Each spring, our school held dances and ice cream socials in order for us to mingle with students from other schools and so parents and faculty could interact in a casual setting. Even though boys were present, the sisters allowed us to attend these events.

The afternoon of the party, Frances, Maria and I stood at the clothes rack deciding what to wear. Frances held a pretty blue dress against my chest.

"You should wear this," she said.

"Catalina, I don't know why you would want to go," Maria said, scraping hangers back and forth.

"Why shouldn't I go?"

"I don't want to sound harsh, but I doubt anyone will ask you to dance. If I were you, I wouldn't go."

Frances punched her fists against her hips. "Why would you say such a hurtful thing?"

"Well, isn't it obvious? She's so dark-skinned." She turned and looked me up and down. "No offense, Caty. I don't mean to sound hurtful. I just don't want you to get your hopes up."

Frances wrinkled her nose at Maria. "Don't listen to her." She pulled me toward the other side of the rack. "She's just jealous. She wants all the boys focused on her tonight, and she sees you as a threat."

"Why would I be a threat?"

"Because you're taller and prettier."

After we had dressed and primped within an inch of our lives, Father and a few sisters herded us out the back door and into several cars. We drove across town to a house owned by one of the school's benefactors. We pulled up to a steel-blue and white mansion nestled within the arms of two mighty oak trees. Spanish moss drowsy-draped across the branches and swayed in the cool breeze as though the whole estate was under water. The large circular driveway was lined with elegant, old-fashioned black lamp posts. Fat green ferns bowed toward us on either side of the cobbled entryway as if we were royalty. The wraparound porch was adorned with iron-laced railings. The light shone through windows that were eyelashed with fringe-dangled curtains.

We entered the foyer and were led down a hallway into a grand ballroom. Music hummed through speakers, and I spotted a man in the corner spinning records. Beside him, a long table brimmed with flower arrangements and crystal punch bowls and trays of cookies. Frances and I poured ourselves some punch and sat down.

The girls all sat in folding chairs along one wall and stared across the barren expanse of a dance floor at the boys in folding chairs against the opposite wall. Finally, one brave boy ventured across the room to ask a girl to dance. A few boys followed suit. A chubby boy with acne came over and asked Frances to dance. The music was nice, and I wanted to dance so badly. I brushed my fingers across my lace gloves and waited a song or two for a boy to come and ask me. By the third song, I got up and refilled my punch glass. Father spotted me and came over.

"Are you having fun?"

"Yes, thank you."

"You should be dancing. Don't be shy."

"I'm not."

Just then, two of the parents walked over and asked Father a question. When he turned to speak with them, I placed my glass on the table and slipped out of the ballroom. I wandered down the hall and found a dark library with floor to ceiling shelves filled with leather bound books. I stepped inside the room and ran my fingers across their spines. A red leather chair was positioned in front of a fireplace. Beside the chair, a pedestal table held a glass ashtray. Inside rested a wood and ivory pipe. The room smelled like rich cherry tobacco and spicy cologne and softly worn leather. They were the kind of sumptuous smells we never had in our house. I took in one last deep breath then ventured back out into the hallway.

I rounded a corner and spotted a group of boys leaning against the hall wall. I watched as they smiled whenever anyone approached them, but as soon as that person had passed, the boys huddled together and snickered. As I approached them, one of them put on a pair of sunglasses.

"Hey, y'all, check this out right here. This Amazon girl, she so black, when I put on the glasses, she disappear."

"Shut up," I hissed.

The boys slapped each other's backs and tossed their heads back in hyena laughter. I didn't understand why they teased me about being black. They were black, too—some even darker than I was. In fact, all the students there were black. My heart rose up and clung to the lining of my tight throat. I could feel hot tears sting my eyes. I dashed into a nearby bathroom and locked the door. I leaned against the countertop and sobbed. After the sorrowful wave had passed, I pulled off my gloves and splashed water on my face. I eventually went back to the ballroom and sat back down.

As it turned out, Maria was right. No one asked me to dance.

Mario had told me about how poorly he had been treated by the other black boys in his orphanage because his skin was darker than theirs. I have never understood colorism, especially within the black community. That's how people thought back then in New Orleans—that the lighter your skin tone was the higher you were seen in the social order. Colorism has always existed. During the time of slavery, lighter-skinned blacks often worked inside the house, whereas a darker-skinned black person was relegated to work in the fields. Even today, magazines often Photoshop black models to make them lighter in order to make them more appealing to the masses. I remember reading somewhere that during Obama's presidential run, media speculated that because he was a light-skinned man, he was more "electable" than if he had been darker-skinned. Colorism is the worst kind of discrimination, because it in itself does not discriminate. It exists everywhere and is present in every culture, and in all races.

I'll never know why no one asked me to dance—if it was because I towered over most of the boys, or because of my dark complexion. Later that night as I laid in bed, I reminded myself that I had bigger fish to fry than fretting about some stupid dance. I was going to be just fine. I had my sights set on graduating and landing a good job. Still, sitting alone against the wall in that ballroom watching everyone else dance hurt me all the same.

Chapter TWENTY-FIVE

That summer, Frances and I were invited to a girls' sleepover camp run by several deacons of the church who worked tirelessly for racial equality. It was the first time that black children were invited to join white children at the camp. Father drove us up there just outside the city on the north shore of Lake Pontchartrain. I stepped out of the car and watched black and white girls play together on a sunny lawn. Beyond the lawn, more girls swam in the lake and rowed canoes. A man approached us and shook Father's hand.

"I'm Deacon Beecher," the man said. He was a white man with short blonde hair and black rimmed glasses. He looked down at me and Frances and smiled. "Welcome. Let's get you two situated."

"Have a nice time," Father said.

We followed Deacon Beecher across camp to a cluster of tents on wooden platforms. He motioned to one of the tents.

"This is where you'll sleep. Drop your things on a bed inside the tent and come down to the lake. Put on a suit if you want to go swimming."

The tent held six wooden cots and six wooden boxes for night stands and little else. Frances dropped her bag on a cot next to the one I chose. Neither of us knew how to swim, so we stayed in our play clothes and headed down to the lake.

I walked along the shore and watched the girls swim. Unlike the experience we had with the white girls in their orphanage swimming by themselves in their pool, the black and white girls at that camp swam together. They seemed to be having fun. Even if I knew how to swim, I'm not sure I would have joined them. It had been drilled into us so many times that it was illegal for the races to mix. Society and public opinion were slowly changing, but I couldn't quite shake the feeling that something bad might befall us at any moment. I found out years later that a similar camp nearby that had hosted both black and white girls that summer found a burning cross on their lawn. Thank goodness nothing like that happened to us, and yet that possibility lingered in the air.

After supper, we all sat on large logs positioned around several campfires. The deacons told ghosts stories, and we made S'mores. Frances and I pierced our marshmallows onto sticks and held them above the flames.

"Frances, watch out," I said. "Your marshmallow is on fire."

"It's okay. I like it that way." She lifted her stick out of the fire and watched the flames lick around the marshmallow. She blew it out, then pulled the charcoal skin off and popped it in her mouth. She thrust the stick back into the fire. "You can get a few good burns out of one marshmallow."

I jammed my stick into the fire and watched my marshmallow burn. I blew it out and pulled the blackened skin off the stick. Frances nodded for me to eat it. I slipped it into my mouth and bit down. The burned bits crunched, and I spit it out.

"That's disgusting."

"No way. It's the best."

"It's like chewing on a piece of coal. It's stuck in my teeth."

"It's an acquired taste."

The deacon laughed. About half the girls sided with me on the virtues of a lightly toasted marshmallow. The other half burned theirs with Frances. Our faces glowed orange from the light of the crackling fire; it flickered against the bellies of the oak leaves above us and magnified our shadows against the tree trunks behind us as though they were dancing. The air was crisp, and the lake was shrouded in a phantomy fog. Canoes were tethered to an invisible dock. I leaned back on the log and watched the bats swoop and flutter between the tree tops like black paper cut outs against a dark navy sky. It was as though I had fallen into a fairy tale.

Toward the end of the week, Frances and I raced bikes up and down a grassy hill. After peddling up, we'd pull up side-by-side at the top then roar down the hill. On one of the trips back up the hill, my wheel must have caught on a rock because the world suddenly tipped sideways. I grabbed at the grass to slow my fall, but my foot became tangled between the wheel and the bike. I landed hard on my side, and pain shot through my leg.

Frances ran to my side and pulled the bike from my ankle.

"Are you hurt? Can you stand up?"

I tried putting weight on my foot, but the pain was too intense.

"I can't. Can you go get help?"

Frances flew down the hill toward the camp. In a minute or two, one of the deacons came up and carried me to the infirmary. The nurse felt along the side of my ankle and shook her head.

"She needs to get an x-ray. I think it's broken."

She secured an ice pack to my ankle, and the deacon drove me to a nearby hospital. They must have phoned the orphanage, because while the doctor wrapped my ankle in a cast, Father came in and sat beside me.

"You okay?" He circled my shoulder with his arm.

"Yeah. Just a dumb fall."

"As soon as it dries, I want to be the first to sign it."

Once the cast had set, Father drove me back to the orphanage, and Sister Celeste helped me to bed. I wasn't unhappy to be back home, but I thought about Frances, and I wished I was back there with her and her fiery marshmallows, watching the bats flit across the starry sky.

That week, because I couldn't stand, I was relegated to sewing duty. I waited all day for Frances to come home from camp. After my darning was finished, I hobbled on my crutches out back to see if she was in the yard. I scanned the girls but didn't see her. I started up the stairs and met Mother coming down.

"Mother, have you seen Frances? I thought she'd be back from camp today."

"She's not here."

"When does she get back?"

"She's not coming back. She doesn't live here anymore. She, Maria, and Vivian were sent to live in a foster home."

"I don't understand."

"This happens to nearly every girl. When they reach a certain age, they're sent to live in a foster home for a time. We feel it's best for the children to experience a foster home so that when they are reunited with their real families, the transition is smoother. The family we use usually takes one or two girls at a time, but they made an exception this time and took Vivian in as well."

"Does that mean their parents have left Cuba? Do you know if my parents got out, too? How can I get in touch with Frances? Can we go visit them?"

"Honestly, Catalina, you ask too many questions."

She slipped passed me and disappeared around the corner.

Chapter TWENTY-SIX

> *"One who knows the Mississippi will promptly aver—not aloud, but to himself—that ten thousand River Commissions, with the mines of the world at their back, cannot tame that lawless stream, cannot curb it or confine it, cannot say to it, Go here, or Go there, and make it obey; cannot save a shore which it has sentenced; cannot bar its path with an obstruction which it will not tear down, dance over, and laugh at."*
> — Mark Twain, *Life on the Mississippi*

In 1717, the French explorer and the then governor of French Louisiana, Jean-Baptiste Le Moyne, Sieur de Bienville, chose the site to build his city *Nouvelle-Orleans* or New Orleans on a natural levee along a sharp crescent-shaped bend in the Mississippi River. He selected the site because it was the highest and driest spot for miles around. He felt sure that it would be safe from tidal surges and hurricanes. His chief royal engineer, Pierre Le Bond de la Tour, did not agree. He tried to in vain to discourage Bienville by pointing out that the area would be prone to frequent flooding. Ignoring the stern warning, Bienville put slaves to work clearing land exactly where he wanted to establish his town. The people of New Orleans have been paying the price for Bienville's pigheadedness ever since.[45]

Most nights, Father Coffey enjoyed the evening news in his room after dinner. One night in early September in 1965, I happened to walk by his door. He and Mother stared furrow-browed at the television.

"A few days ago, Hurricane Betsy was north of San Juan," Father said. "It looped north toward the Carolinas and weakened, but it headed south and strengthened again. It looks as though it's headed for south Florida."

"Should we be worried?" Mother asked.

"Not yet. It's still pretty far away. Are the pantries stocked?"

"Always are."

The following Monday, Labor Day, Father and a few of the sisters loaded us into cars after breakfast, and we headed for the beach one last time before school started. The grey-green water of Lake Pontchartrain was warm and calm. The clear, high sky was painfully blue. As the girls swam, I gathered sea shells and made sand castles near the shore. Father spent the day slouched in a beach chair with a transistor radio in his lap listening to weather updates.

The next morning, Father drove us to school in shifts. I was anxious to see Frances. After he dropped me off, I put my book bag down and planted myself outside on the school steps waiting for her. I scanned the faces of the girls as they filed passed me. I stood alone on the steps well after the last girl had gone inside. I realized that Frances wasn't coming. I didn't know if I'd ever see her again. That thought made my insides heavy. I picked up my book bag and went inside. After school, I walked home alone.

The following night after dinner, we gathered in Father's room to watch the news. The weatherman pointed to the wide, mean radar swirl on the wall behind him.

"It's strengthened to a category 3," Sister Celeste said.

"It looks like it might make landfall somewhere in the Florida Keys," Father said.

"If that happens, then where will it go?" I asked.

"There's a good chance it will move into the Gulf."

"You think it could hit us?" Sister Fabian asked.

Father shrugged. "God only knows where she'll go, but yes, she very well could hit us."

As it turned out, Hurricane Betsy did make landfall in Key Largo on September 8th. She quickly moved into the warm waters of the Gulf of

Mexico and shifted to the north-northwest and intensified to a category 4 storm.

On the morning of Sept 9th, the storm set her sights on the Louisiana coast. We all helped Father and the sisters to prepare the house. We brought in all the toys, bikes, tables, chairs, and swings from the yard. Father trimmed tree branches and brought in the statue of Mary from the front yard and stashed her in a closet. He and the sisters pulled the cars into the garage and into the back yard close to the house.

After the last bike had been wheeled through the back door, I stood in the back yard for a moment. The sky was cloudless and light blue. It was eerily quiet—the tree branches were motionless, and there wasn't a bird in the sky. It was as if the whole world held its breath.

"Come inside, Caty," Mother said.

"Yes, ma'am."

That afternoon, we played in the playroom while Father and the sisters hovered around the TV. Time dragged as we waited for the hurricane to hit. After dinner, the skies darkened and the winds picked up. We all crowded into Father's room and watched the weather reports. The radar showed that the storm had set its sights on New Orleans.

"We now have a mandatory evacuation of Eastern New Orleans," the weatherman said. "Hurricane warnings are now up from Galveston, TX to the Mississippi River Delta."

"I know it's early, but I want you girls to go to bed and try to get some sleep," Mother said. "I have a feeling it will be a long night."

We went to our rooms, and I laid on my belly and looked out the window. Although I had lived my whole life on an island in the Caribbean Sea, I had never experienced a hurricane, so I didn't know what to expect. The wind hollered through the trees, snapping branches. A sudden gust pushed hard against the window, and I swooped under the covers. Sometime in the middle of the night, Mother came to our room.

"Girls, get up and come with me. Bring your pillow and blanket."

Father was in the hall gathering everyone together.

"I want you all to come with me."

"Are we going to be all right?" one of the younger girls asked.

"Yes, but I want to make sure we ride this out smartly. The storm is coming in from the south, so I want us to gather together in the middle of the hall toward the northern part of the house. I want us all to stay on the third floor in case there's any flooding. It might get a little loud and rocky, but we'll get through this."

We hunkered down in the hall buried in blankets and pillows as though we were all at sleepover camp. Sister Celeste brought up baskets of sandwiches and apples. Mother handed out a few flashlights.

"We have candles here, too, just in case the power is cut," Sister Fabian said.

No sooner had she said that than the lights went out. She lit glass jar candles and placed them at intervals throughout the hall.

"The phones are out as well," Mother said, coming from her office.

Just before midnight, Hurricane Betsy barreled ashore like a 125-mph-freight train. The National Weather Service reported that the hurricane, which had been a category 4 storm, weakened slightly to a category 3 just before coming ashore about 100 miles south of New Orleans at Grand Isle.

Throughout the night, the building swayed from side to side as though it might blow over at any moment. Can you image the strength of the wind being able to move a three-story brick building? It's a wonder that it didn't come down. At one point, I looked up and saw a crack open in the ceiling and roadmap its way down the hall. Wooden beams squealed. I was sure the roof would fly off, but it held.

No one cried out or whimpered or even appeared frightened, even during the worst of the storm. I'm sure many of us were terrified on the inside, but Father was so calm and authoritative. He kept telling us that everything was going to be all right, and because he was so steady and reassuring, we absolutely believed him. We huddled together in the hallway until morning. Finally, Father stood and stretched his back.

"It sounds like the winds have died down," he said. "Stay here while Mother and I go downstairs and make sure everything is safe."

After a few minutes, he called up the stairs.

"It's okay. There's no damage to the house. You can come downstairs, but stay inside and don't drink the water."

We went downstairs and got dressed. Aunt Rose, who lived nearby, was already in the kitchen. She had fired up the gas stove and was perking coffee and had whipped up a batch of biscuits for us. As Mother and the sisters served us breakfast, Aunt Rose stood in the dining room doorway with a puzzled look on her face.

"What is it, Rose?" Mother asked.

"There's something I think you need to see," she motioned toward the back door.

As Mother and Father went to the back door, we all stumbled over to the window to take a look. That's when I noticed the extent of the damage done to the back yard. The heavy tree branches were everywhere and had fallen onto the swing set and crushed the back fence. And then I saw them. Wet, mud-caked people had formed a long line outside our back door all the way back behind the garage. Mother and Father went out and greeted them. Some people were crying; others appeared shell-shocked. As Mother and Father turned to come back inside, we raced to back our seats.

"Girls, finish up quickly." Mother stood in the middle of the dining room. "I want you girls on this side of the room to carry the tables and chairs out to the back yard. You girls on this side of the room will go to the kitchen. You'll help Aunt Rose make sandwiches and get coffee out to those poor people."

While Father and some of the men moved branches out of the way, we carried the tables and chairs out back and invited people to sit down. The sisters brought out fresh towels and bandages. We fed them and listened to them. Most of the city was under water, in some cases up to 16 feet of water. Levees for the Mississippi River Gulf Outlet along Florida Avenue and on both sides of the Industrial Canal levee had breached—some people insisting that they had been dynamited—allowing an ocean of water to wash through the nearby Lower Ninth Ward. We found out later that Hurricane Betsy had wiped out entire communities in St. Bernard and Plaquemines Parishes. Over six thousand homes were flooded. We were lucky because our part of town was slightly elevated, enough to save us.

The water in the city stood for more than a week. Hundreds of ships, tugs and barges were sunk or driven aground from New Orleans to Baton Rouge. Eleven shipwrecks blocked 30 miles of the Mississippi River. One barge, which contained enough chlorine to kill tens of thousands of people if released sank in 60 feet of water near the University of Louisiana campus. After weeks of frantic searching, the barge was finally located and refloated without incident.

When all was said and done, seventy-six people had lost their lives. The water reached the eaves of the houses in some neighborhoods and well over most of the one-story homes. Many people drowned in their attics trying to escape the rising water. This was the first hurricane in the United States to have accrued damages over $1 billion and soon garnered the nicknamed Billion Dollar Betsy. Because it was so deadly and devastating, the name Betsy was retired from the hurricane list and replaced with the name Blanche.

And every morning, the people lined up outside our back door. One morning as I took a tray of donuts out to the people, I saw that Maria was floating between the tables pouring coffee. I ran over to her.

"Maria, you're here. How are you? How's Frances? And Vivian?"

"We're okay. I was given permission to come by and help. Frances is okay. Vivian, well, let's just say, Vivian is surviving."

"What do you mean?"

Maria pulled me off to the side and lowered her voice. "Our foster parents, the Malgrins, are nice enough to me and Frances, but I don't think they like Vivian much. They scold her all the time and make her do most of the chores."

"Why? What did she do?"

"Nothing, that's just it. They never had children of their own, so they take care of girls for the money. They usually only take in one or two at a time, but this time, they took Vivian in too, for the extra money. I have a feeling that it was Mr. Malgrin's idea, and that Mrs. Malgrin wasn't consulted, and she's none too happy about having to stretch her meals."

Just then, Mother came out back with a tray of sandwiches. She gave us an icy glare and wagged her head for us to get back to work. I followed Maria back to the tables and passed out donuts. I was far-off thinking of Frances and of Vivian being scolded when a young white man grabbed my arm and snapped me back from where I had been thinking. His clothes were filthy, and black dirt had caked under his finger nails. He looked up to me with wet, vacant eyes that had seen way too much terrible.

"I want to thank you, young lady. Thank you very much."

"You're very welcome."

He released my arm, and his eyes floated down to his coffee cup before the tears could spill. I handed him another donut.

"Take two."

He kept his eyes on his cup and nodded. Seeing that man's suffering made me understand that my troubles were nothing. Nothing. And that I was blessed. After that wake-up call, I made sure to look everyone that I was serving straight in the eye. Seeing those people, some voicing their gratitude, others simply too inside themselves to do so, profoundly changed me. It was weeks before our power was restored, yet every morning, we got up and helped the many who came to us.

I'll never forget their utter hopelessness at having lost everything. There was no distinction between race—equal number of blacks and whites huddled together in our back yard. We welcomed them and fed them all. It's strange that in the wake of that horrid disaster, I was shown the greatest lesson—in the end, there is no "us" or "them," but only "we."

Chapter TWENTY-SEVEN

"How would you like to go to the movies?" Mother asked me one afternoon.

"Sure."

"They're playing The Sound of Music at the Saenger Theatre."

"Isn't that a whites-only theater?"

"They want to integrate it, so we thought you'd like to be one of the ones to do so."

I blinked at her for a moment. "Why me?"

"Would you like to go to the movies or not?"

I found out later that they chose me because when we Cuban girls were asked to eat at the Woolworth's counter, we were very well behaved. Since that went off without a hitch, they (whoever *they* were) knew there would be no drama. I was the only girl to go that night, because Maria, Frances and Vivian were in the foster home. I was the only Cuban girl left at the orphanage.

Besides Mr. Ramos, we were assigned another Cuban social worker to our orphanage. Her name was Eva Consuegra. She was a young, curvy light caramel-colored woman with dark brown hair that cupped at her shoulders and giant brown pony eyes. Mother arranged it so that she would accompany me to the movies. Miss Consuegra came to the orphanage that afternoon wearing a dark blue dress, high heels, and pill box hat. She wore blue eye shadow and fuchsia lipstick, and her cheeks were rouged up as if someone had double slapped her. Mother, Miss Consuegra and I headed downstairs to the clothes rack.

"I'd like to wear my Easter dress, if I may," I said. I pulled a carnation pink dress off the rack. It had a lace bodice and a satin bow at the waist. The woman whose name I can't remember bought it for me the previous Easter at Maison Blanche.

"Excellent choice," Mother said.

After I showered, I slipped into my dress, pulled on a pair of panty hose and stepped into white patent leather pumps with a low, elegant heel. They took me out to the beauty parlor out back where they yanked, ironed, glossed, and shiny-new-pennied my hair into soft flowing curls—the type white women wore. My kinky black hair didn't know what had hit it. Miss Consuegra and Mother spun me around in the beauty parlor chair to face the mirror.

"Whoa." I stared at my reflection, open mouthed.

"You look incredible—so grown up," Miss Consuegra said. "You ready to go?"

"Yes, ma'am."

We donned our coats and sauntered out to the station wagon. Miss Consuegra and I glided into the back seat. Father adjusted the rearview mirror and smiled at us. He pulled out of the driveway, and drove 15 minutes to the theater on Canal Street and N. Rampart Street on the rim of the French Quarter. He pulled up to the sidewalk in front of the theater and threw an elbow over the seat to look straight at me.

"You have fun tonight." "I will."

We stepped out of the car and filed into the long line to buy tickets. When we got to the ticket booth, Miss Consuegra went ahead of me. After she purchased her ticket, she stood beside me. The white woman in the glass booth smiled at me.

"One, please."

I slid money into the slot, and she pushed the ticket out toward me.

"Enjoy the show."

Miss Consuegra beamed. I had no idea that that simple transaction had just made history. Other people around me may have pointed at me, or made comments, or even taken pictures. I was oblivious to it all. I was just so excited to see the show.

The Saenger Theatre is one of the oldest theaters in New Orleans. It was built in 1927 by Julian and Abe Saenger and opened on February 4, 1927. The 4,000-seat theatre took three years to build and cost a whopping $2.5 million dollars.[46]

We walked inside and upstairs to the balcony. Both walls to the right and left inside the theater were adorned with enormous façades in what architect Emile Weil had hoped would conjure up images of an Italian Baroque courtyard. It was billed as an acre of seats in a garden of Florentine splendor. He had installed 150 lights in the ceiling to mimic the constellations in the night sky. I found out later that the theater also had special effects machines that could project images of moving clouds, sunrises, and sunsets across the walls and ceiling of the theater.

Julian Saenger sold his theater in 1929 to Paramount Publix for $10 million dollars. In 1964, the large balcony was walled off in order to form two smaller spaces so they could showcase the new wide-screen movies…and to charge more money, of course. The upstairs theater was dubbed the Saenger Orleans.[47] It was the grandest thing I had ever seen.

We wiggled out of our coats and sat down. Miss Consuegra watched me run my fingers along the plush velvet seats.

"They're so soft," I said. "It's like stroking a red crew cut."

I took in the ceiling lights, the details of the façades, and all the brilliant colors. I drank it in, every little bit. I noticed on the other side of the balcony, an older black woman came in and took her seat. We were the only two black people in the theater. I leaned over the balcony and watched the others, the men in their three-piece suits and the ladies in their fancy dresses and heels, file in and take their seats. It was clear, this was no country bumpkin affair.

After most were settled in their seats, the lights dimmed and the thick crimson curtains parted like the Red Sea. The music swelled and suddenly, the grey and white snowy peaks of Austria rose up on the enormous screen. Then, Julie Andrews appeared with outstretched arms and spun herself on that mountainside, and I experienced jaw-hung-open enchantment.

After the movie ended, Miss Consuegra and I stood in line with the rest of the white women to use the restroom. Again, me simply going to the bathroom with the whites was history making. We left the theater and waited on the curb for Father. We were surrounded by waves of people leaving the theater, many of them still humming tunes that refused to escape their memories too quickly. Fur-clad and pearl-dangled, the women huddled into the crooks of their men's elbows, both of them stamping their feet to keep warm waiting for a cab.

It wasn't the first movie that I had seen in a theater, but it was certainly the most impressive, and not just because the movie was marvelous. It was because the entire evening was an event—getting to dress up and see all those fancy people, and me being welcomed to be a part of that experience. I may have made history that night, but I remember it as being one of the nicest evenings I had spent in New Orleans. It was lovely because I wasn't seen as less-than or extra-special. I was simply an easy part of the crowd.

Chapter TWENTY-EIGHT

At Christmastime that year, Elaine Lugo, the older girl at the orphanage who had chaperoned me whenever I met with Pete, became engaged to her longtime boyfriend, Nelson. She was in the parlor showing us her ring when Father walked in.

"Father, did you hear, Elaine got engaged," Martha said.

Father nodded. "Girls, why don't you go to bed. I'd like to speak with Elaine."

We left the room, but hovered just outside on the stairs and strained our ears to hear what Father had to say.

"You don't approve," Elaine said.

"It's not that I don't approve. I like Nelson. He seems like a very decent boy. I have concerns about his health. He's young, but has already had heart problems, not to mention his diabetes. I'm just afraid that if you marry him and start a family, he might not be around to support you, and you'd be stuck."

"I love him, and I want to marry him."

"I know you do. I'm just saying these things because I care. It wouldn't be right if I didn't voice my concerns. I think of you all as my daughters. What kind of a father would I be if I didn't put up a fuss for my daughter?"

"Then as my father, would you give me away?"

There was silence that lasted for ages, and we all held our breath. Finally, Father spoke. "I'd be honored."

We hush-high-fived each other and tiptoed up the stairs to bed. I thought of Elaine while I got ready for bed. I was so happy for her. She was about to leave and marry the man she loved and start a family of her own. I envied her, too. I hadn't had any romances in my life until that point. It's nice to have girlfriends, but there's something special about a boy appreciating you in a tender way. I hoped there might be a man out there somewhere who would love me, who would caress the back of my neck with his fingertips, throwing sparks. But after that social where those boys teased me and no one asked me to dance, I got to thinking that I might not ever find a man to marry me, let alone love me. I might not ever have a family of my own.

One afternoon that winter, Mother found me playing dominos with Martha in the playroom after school.

"Catalina, may I have a word with you in my office?"

"Have I done something wrong?"

"No, why would you say that?" "Because you've never asked me to meet you in your office before."

"You're not in trouble. Now, come with me."

I followed her into her office. She sat behind her desk then swiveled sideways positioning herself in front of a typewriter. I sat down and waited for her to finish typing a letter. She finally swiveled her chair back toward me.

"Catalina, it's time for you to leave the orphanage and live at the foster home."

"Please don't make me go there. This is my home."

"I'm afraid you have no choice."

"Wait a minute. If I'm going to the foster home, that means I'll soon be with my family, isn't that right?"

"I can't get into the specifics, but I can tell you that Mario is being sent to a foster home as well. His new home is just around the corner from yours. Now, go down to the clothes rack and pick out a few outfits to take with you."

I waited for her to give me a smile or wink or anything that might give me a clue about what she knew about my family, but she kept her poker face.

"What about Maria and Frances and Vivian?" I asked.

"Maria and Frances are gone. They flew to Miami this morning to be with their parents who arrived in Florida last week."

I sat for a moment without saying anything. There it was. I would never see Frances again. Our friendship that had been linked by politics and fate and had simply scattered away like frost-coated leaves. That fact washed over me like a thick muddy wave. Of course, I was happy that she and Maria were finally with their parents, but still, I felt hollow.

"What about Vivian?"

"Vivian is still at the foster home. You'll pack your things and leave here tomorrow."

I left Mother's office and drifted through the halls. I took a deep breath and filled my lungs with Aunt Rose's strong chicory that flowed up from the kitchen like a warm black current in the air, the sharp lemon oil on the wooden stair banisters, and everywhere, the tang of pine cleaner. I made my way to the chapel and sat in the dark for a while in the familiar gaze of the Virgin statue watching the flames flicker in the sanctuary votive candles. The air was perfumed with candle wax and incense and the dusty smell of the hymnals. All those scents mingled together to create a sense of home for me. In the three and a half years that I had been at the orphanage, it *had* become my home. I tried, but I couldn't remember how my own house smelled back in Cuba.

I picked out an armful of clothes from the rack and wound my way back to my room. Mother had placed a cardboard box on my bed. With something more than care, I packed my things into the box then set it on the floor. I didn't feel like eating supper, so I laid down on my bed one last time. I was on the cusp of thirteen, just a month shy of moving into the teenager's room. I had slept in that bed since I had arrived. It had seemed so big to me at first, as though I might be swallowed by the blankets, but as I laid there studying the ceiling, I brushed my toes along the footboard. I closed my eyes and listened to the sounds of the house—the shoes scuffing against the wood floors, the laughter and the music and the chatter in English, my language now.

It made sense in a way, for me to have left the orphanage when I did. Like a farmer cutting down the older trees to make room for the new ones to grow, I needed to go to make room for the new girls that would come. I had a chance to move forward, to prepare to be with my family again. Martha and Paulette and the rest of the Cadre sisters did not. They would have to stay there until they were old enough to get a job and be on their own or marry.

I was happy to know that there was a good chance that Mario and I would be with our family again, but a sudden current of sorrow rose up and unspooled. In that place where hopes and fears are met, I was overcome with a mixture of dread, and a profound ache, and a desolate homesickness for my far-off and half-forgotten family. I longed to be with them, but the truth was, after all that time, they had become strangers to me. I tried hard to remember every detail of what they looked like or what their voices sounded like, but my memory had muddied the way the sharp edges dull in an old photograph. I let out a long mournful moan like an eerie whale song and let the tears sticky my cheeks until blessed sleep finally found me.

The next morning, Tuesday, February 15th, I woke in darkness and watched as the navy sky gradually faded to shades of lighter blue as though God, perched in his great armchair, leaned over and trickled celestial milk into the heavens. The sun rose one ribbon of light at a time and warmed the bellies of the leaves high up in the treetops. I said a quick prayer of gratitude for the orphanage and those people who had fed and taught and protected me, then got dressed, picked up my box and went downstairs. Father was in the kitchen, leaning against the counter, sipping his coffee.

"You ready?" he asked.

"Yes, sir."

"Did you get a chance to say goodbye to Aunt Rose and the sisters and the girls?"

"No. If I don't say goodbye, they would still be a part of my life as though they were in the next room."

"Understood." He placed his coffee cup in the sink. "Let's do this."

He motioned for me to hand him my box, and I followed him out the back door. I eased into the back seat of the station wagon. Someone told me once that it was bad luck to look back, so I kept my eyes forward as we pulled out onto the street.

We drove about 15 minutes across town and turned into the driveway of a plain white house in the middle of the block. A short, middle-aged white man stood behind the banister of the front porch and waved to us as though he was on the deck of a great ship. He wore black framed glasses, and his light brown hair horseshoed around his head just above the ears. The long thin locks swooped up and over his bald noggin in a fancy swirl culminating in a feathery question mark just above his forehead. Father and I got out, and the man came down the walkway toward us.

"Bienvenida Catalina Miranda, this is Mr. Jean-François Malgrin," Father said. "He and his wife, Clotille, will take very good care of you."

"Hello, sir. Please, call me Catalina."

He shook my hand. "Pleased to meet you, Catalina. Let's get you settled."

Mr. Malgrin took my box from Father and headed toward the front door. I turned and fell into Father's arms and hugged him tightly.

"You'll be just fine. Remember, we're a phone call away."

I tried to say something to him, but my throat squeezed shut, so I just nodded and turned away. I fought hard not to turn back and look at him. Instead, I waited at the open front door with my back to the driveway and listened to the station wagon pull onto the street. After the sound of the engine had faded away, I stepped inside.

Mrs. Malgrin stood in the living room with her hands clasped in front of her stomach. She was a heavy-set white woman with short, mouse-colored curls. She had made an attempt at taming her hair nest with two rose-shaped barrettes on either side of her face, but the chaos in the back looked as though it had been combed with salad tongs. Large pink arms poked from a striped maroon and cream-colored dress.

The walls of the living room had been papered in mauve and cream stripes. Had it not been for the breadth of her three dimensionality, she might have blended right into the walls.

"Welcome, Catalina."

Vivian stepped around a corner into the living room, and I gasped. Once voluptuous, her too-big-clothes drooped off her frail body. Dark half moons sagged under her eyes. Mrs. Malgrin motioned for her to enter the room.

"You know Vivian, of course."

"Yes, thank you."

Mr. Malgrin entered the living room from a hallway and sat down in a plum-colored chair next to the fireplace.

"I placed your box on top of your bed," Mr. Malgrin said. He crossed his legs and tented a newspaper in front of his face. Mrs. Malgrin narrowed her eyes and shot a furious glance in his direction, then lifted her nose toward the ceiling.

"Let *me* give you the five-cent tour." She gave with a Vanna White arm swoop. "This here's the living room."

An overstuffed plum-colored couch and chair sat opposite Mr. Malgrin. Their arms were draped with lace doilies. In front of the fireplace at Mr. Malgrin's feet lay a blood red Persian-type area rug. The rest of the floor was carpeted the color of oatmeal. Above the mantel, there was an antique wooden clock. Porcelain tchotchkes perched on every available surface. In the middle of the coffee table in front of the sofa lay a huge lace doily. It had been starched and the edges lifted into ruffles as though Shakespeare had left his collar behind. In the middle of the doily sat a glass candy dish that cupped sugary green gum drops.

I followed Mrs. Malgrin and Vivian into the kitchen where the maroon theme continued. The dining room opened up beyond the gold-flecked L-shaped linoleum counter where an oval table was surrounded by four high-back chairs. She motioned for me and Vivian to follow her back through the living room into a grey-flowered hallway and up the stairs.

"Your room is here," she pointed. I paused to peek inside the room and saw two beds, dressers and pretty lace curtains.

"And this is our bedroom," she said. "The master bath is in the rear of our bedroom."

Mrs. Malgrin floated back out into the hallway. I leaned close to Vivian.

"If this is the master bath, where's the other one," I whispered.

"That's it, just the one," she whispered back.

We joined Mrs. Malgrin in the hallway. "Catalina, you can unpack your things, and then the two of you come down for lunch."

We entered our bedroom and sat down on our beds. Mrs. Malgrin smiled at us from the door. As soon as Mrs. Malgrin disappeared, I turned to Vivian.

"Vivian—"

She put her finger to her lips to quiet me. She shook her head and motioned toward the door. Apparently, Mrs. Malgrin liked to linger in the hallway. Vivian laid down and closed her eyes. I wanted to ask her so many questions, but it was clear she wasn't ready to talk.

After lunch, Mrs. Malgrin asked us to go back upstairs and play in our room for a while. We each grabbed a book from the shelf against the wall in our room and settled onto our beds. Not long after, Mrs. Malgrin screeched up from the bottom of the stairs.

"Vivian, come down here, please."

We both came down and found Mrs. Malgrin in the kitchen with her fists on her hips. She turned and faced me.

"Is your name Vivian?"

"No ma'am."

"Then I suggest you march yourself back up to your room."

I crept back through the living room and crouched on the stairs so I could see into the kitchen. Mr. Malgrin was still sitting in the living room. He glanced at me over the top of the paper then continued reading.

"Do you see anything out of place?" Mrs. Malgrin asked Vivian.

"I'm not sure. I cleaned everything like you asked."

She pointed to a bowl of oranges on the counter top.

"What about this bowl looks different to you?"

"Um, I had an orange."

Mrs. Malgrin backhanded Vivian hard across the face. I cried out in surprise and quickly covered my mouth. I looked to Mr. Malgrin to help Vivian, but he didn't seem to hear what was going on in the kitchen.

"Did I say that you could have an orange? Don't you dare take so much as a burnt match from this house without asking me. Do I make myself clear?"

"Yes, ma'am."

"Now go to your room."

I made a beeline up the stairs to our bedroom. Vivian entered with her eyes to the floor. A hand print bloomed rosy red on her cheek.

"I'm so sorry that happened to you."

She shook her head and flopped face down onto her bed. I knew right then and there that I had to watch my every move around the Malgrins.

Chapter TWENTY-NINE

That weekend, I found St. Timothy's Catholic Church a few blocks away from the Malgrin's house, and every Sunday from then on, I made it a point to go to mass there no matter the weather. I enjoyed that time by myself. It gave me a chance to pray and be with my thoughts. It became my lifeline to hope. St. Timothy's was segregated, so I slipped in after the white priest and altar boys processed up the center aisle just as the opening hymn started. I sat quietly in the back pew, never singing or praying out loud so as not to call any attention to myself. I listened to the priest speak of Christ and brotherly love and watched the backs of all those white heads nod in agreement. During the Prayer of the Faithful part of the Mass, I watched the lector step up to the pulpit and read a list of intentions.

"For world leaders, that they work together to promote peace and justice for all, let us pray to the Lord. Lord, hear our prayer."

Yeah, peace and justice for all. I had a feeling that if one or two of those white folks turned around and saw a black girl sitting in their white church, peace and justice would fly straight out the stained-glass window. At the end of the Mass as the priest stood to give the final blessing, I slipped back out the front door, down the steps to the sidewalk and hurried away from the church.

The following week was Ash Wednesday. I stood at the kitchen sink beside Mrs. Malgrin one night after dinner while she washed the dishes and I dried. As I reached into the rinse water for a clean plate to dry, I cleared my throat.

"Mrs. Malgrin, can I ask you a question?"

"Go on."

"This Wednesday is Ash Wednesday. I was wondering, do you think I could go to the orphanage on Tuesday to celebrate Mardi Gras with the girls? They all go to the parade and get to sit in their stands right there on the parade route."

"You'll have to ask Mother Fidelis. You may use the telephone."

I hadn't anticipating having to speak with Mother Fidelis. I dried my hands and picked up the phone. As soon as I heard Mother's voice on the other end, all the water suddenly evaporated from my mouth and magically appeared in my palms.

"Hi Mother, it's Catalina. I asked Mrs. Malgrin if I could go to the parade on Tuesday with the girls at the orphanage."

"I don't think that's a good idea," she said. "I fear if I let you come, it will only encourage you to hold onto the past. You're there because you need to look to the future."

"But if I'll be with my family soon as you hinted, this would be my very last change to celebrate Mardi Gras with my friends." Then, pouring it on thick, "Besides, who knows if I'll ever be able to come back to New Orleans to experience this rich tradition?"

There was silence on the other end of the phone. I could hear her shuffling papers.

"All right. You can come over, but only for one day, Tuesday."

"Can I come over early and get my hair done at the beauty parlor with the rest of the girls?"

She sighed. "Yes, but mark my words, this will be your last visit."

"Yes, ma'am. Thank you."

On Tuesday morning, Mr. Malgrin drove me to the orphanage. I came in the back door and said hello to Aunt Rose. I spied the King Cake on the counter, and she cut me a slice.

"They're all out getting their hair done."

"Thank you."

I hurried out to the beauty parlor. Martha and Paulette were there as well as the older girls and a few new young faces. I slid into the chair next to Martha to wait my turn.

"How are you?" I asked.

"Fine."

"Well, what's new?"

"Nothing."

Nothing. It was strange. We sat next to each other and had nothing to say. I had known Martha for three and a half years—lived with her, and slept right next to her, and we always had something to say. For the first time, I felt as though I no longer belonged. I had only been gone a week, and although no one treated me any different per se, I felt as though I was no longer welcome.

I got my hair done, and we all walked to the parade. We climbed the risers and took our seats. We passed around King Cake and cheered as the floats rambled by. I had a nice time, but it just wasn't the same. I guess that saying is true after all. However, much as you may want to, you can never go back.

The following week, I was allowed to visit Mario at his foster home. I walked three blocks and found the yellow and white house with green awnings toward the end of the street. Mario's foster mother answered the door. She was a slender Filipina woman with long brown hair.

"You must be Mario's sister, Catalina. I'm Mrs. Guzman."

"Pleased to meet you."

"Likewise. Please come in."

I followed her through the living room to the kitchen. Mario was sitting at a small round table sipping sweet iced tea. He rose when he saw me.

"Catalina, would you like some iced tea, dear?" Mrs. Guzman said.

"Yes, ma'am."

She poured me a tall glass of tea then left the room.

"So, how's it going?"

"You know when you sit at a campfire and the smoke follows you no matter where you move? They say that smoke follows the fool. Well, for some reason, bad times follow me."

"I don't understand."

Mario strained his neck to see where Mrs. Guzman got herself, then leaned over the table toward me.

"I was beaten in the orphanage for being too black. Well, here, I get beaten just because."

"What?"

He unbuttoned his shirt and showed me his neck and his right shoulder. The whole area was swollen and purple. He sat back and rebuttoned his shirt.

"Whenever Mr. Guzman gets liquored up, which is pretty often, he comes home late, furious at his sorry life, looking for any excuse to take out his frustrations at not having a job, or fighting with the law, or because the day ends in Y."

He took another sip of tea and cleared his throat. "In the beginning, I'd hear him come in late at night and clomp up the stairs. Their bedroom door would slam. That's when the shouting started. The fight carried on until Mrs. Guzman screamed. It'd end with a thump—assumingly her body hitting the floor, the night stand, or wall."

"Jesus, Mario."

"Yeah, I'd come down in the morning, and she'd be at the stove stirring eggs trying to hide the fresh bruise beneath a lock of hair. A few nights ago, I heard him coming in. Instead of lying in bed like a coward, I got up and stood at the top of the stairs.

'Get outta my way, nigger' he said.

When I didn't budge, he wailed on me."

I shook my head. "You can't let this happen."

"Better me than her."

"Mario, you need to tell someone about this."

"And now who do you suggest I call? The police? That's rich."

"Your social worker maybe? Someone has to know about this."

He shook his head. "I don't want to make waves. I don't think you understand, Caty. The South isn't changing fast enough. Forget Civil Rights, if I, a very dark-skinned man, raise a hand or make a fuss with Mr. Guzman, a very light-skinned man, he can call the cops and have me thrown in jail for a long time. And if such a case ever went to trial, we both know what the outcome would be. We're so close to leaving, I can't take any chances."

After about a half hour of small talk, Mrs. Guzman came back in the kitchen.

"How are you doing? Can I get you more tea?"

"No thank you, ma'am," I said. "I have to be getting back."

Mario walked me out through the living room to the front door. I wanted so badly to hug him, but I knew that would upset him.

"I'll see you again soon," I said.

He nodded and closed the door behind me. As it turned out, I only saw him once more. That afternoon, he came to visit me at the Malgrin's with a bruise below his left eye. He didn't have to tell me that it was Mr. Guzman's handiwork. We both understood that we could no longer visit each other—we'd both be too troubled by what couldn't be changed.

Chapter THIRTY

After two weeks at the foster home, Mrs. Malgrin made an announcement at dinner.

"Vivian, Mr. Ramos is coming by this evening to speak with you."

"Is there something wrong?"

"Well, we'll just have to see."

We ate the rest of our dinner in silence. After dinner, we all gathered in the living room to watch TV, but I don't think Vivian or I could tell you what was on even if someone had held a gun to our heads. We sat wordlessly together as one might wait with her friend in an oncologist's office waiting for dreaded test results.

There came a knock on the door, and Mr. Ramos was ushered in. We all shook hands, then Mrs. Malgrin escorted him and Vivian into the dining room to talk. I tried to peer around the corner, but Mrs. Malgrin had other ideas.

"Catalina, go to your room."

I sat on my bed trying to read a book, until finally, Vivian came up and closed the bedroom door.

"Well?"

"I'm going home. Mr. Ramos said that my parents were able to leave Cuba. They flew into New Orleans a week ago. My father got a job, and they rented a house not too far from here. I'm going to leave here tomorrow to be with them."

"If they've been here a week, why didn't they tell you earlier?"

"I guess they wanted to wait until my parents were settled."

"I'm thrilled for you."

"Don't be. Don't get me wrong, I don't want to spend another day here, but I'm not completely thrilled with my parents."

"How can you say that?"

"I never wanted to leave Cuba in the first place. I begged them not to send me, but they didn't listen to me. I tried everything to convince them to let me stay with them. I'm their only child. What if something happened to me, or them?"

"But it didn't. You're fine, and they're out. You're all free."

"Am I fine? Being here in New Orleans has changed me and not for the better. It's hardened me. I don't like the person I've become. I never knew hate before I came here. How can I just shake that off?"

I knew what she meant. I had changed, too. I was only twelve years old, but was more suspicious and cynical than many of the adults I knew. The shine had been buffed off the young naïve little apple.

I helped Vivian pack her things, then we both slipped under the covers and turned off the lights. The following morning, I woke to find that Vivian's bed was made and she had already gone. I said a prayer for her and her parents, wishing only the best for her.

At first, I thought Mother had made a mistake by sending us to live at the foster home before we were sent back to our families, but over time, I saw that she had been right. Shrewd providence revealed itself slowly and deliberately. The sisters were busy running the orphanage and had no time to teach each one of us what we needed to learn in order to become independent. Mrs. Malgrin took me to the grocery store and taught me how to shop for food and plan for meals. She had me cook and clean. She even showed me how to balance a check book. I was encouraged to take small trips on the bus to go shopping for myself. They gave me a sense of independence, strength, and confidence that I hadn't known before.

I eventually understood how important it was for us to become independent, because our families would have just arrived to this country and may not speak the language or be familiar with the customs. Not only were the Malgrins teaching me, they knew in turn that I would be able to help my family navigate in their new homeland.

I wish I could say that things turned out as well for Mario, but he wasn't as lucky. With Mr. Guzman's tight-fisted rule, there was only so much that Mrs. Guzman could teach him. She wasn't allowed a car or extra pocket money, so she couldn't easily take him places. And knowing Mario and his machismo way of thinking, I can't imagine that he would have willingly asked to be taught how to shop or cook or clean.

After the abuse that he experienced both at his orphanage and his foster home, Mario changed profoundly. Even years later, on his best days, Mario was quiet and brooding—on his worst, bitter and physically abusive. He was known to beat his women. That's not how we were raised. Even when Pipo and Mima were very angry at each other or with us, neither of them struck us. Mario learned that reproachful behavior in New Orleans and carried it with him the rest of his days.

Chapter THIRTY-ONE

One evening, there came a knock on the door. Mrs. Malgrin opened the door and showed Mr. Ramos in.

"Hi, Catalina. Can we talk?"

I grabbed his hand and dragged him into the dining room. I didn't wait for him to take a seat.

"Well?" I asked.

"Well, your family is out of Cuba. They all got out."

"All of them?"

"I don't know how he managed it, but Pete and his wife, Caridad, were able to get your mother, Nené, Lydia, Lazaro, and his wife, Victoria, and their two sons plane tickets out of Cuba. They all flew out last week and now live in Manhattan."

"New York City?"

"Yes. It's unheard of, but Pete did it. Pete bought plane tickets for you and Mario. You'll leave here tomorrow afternoon and be with your family tomorrow night."

I felt all the heaviness and anguish that had been buried deep inside me for so long suddenly rush from my body as though a bottle of champagne had been uncorked.

"I don't know what to say. I dreamed about this day, but I never really thought it would come true."

"It's true. Now, you need to pack. I'll see you tomorrow."

After Mr. Ramos left, Mrs. Malgrin followed me upstairs with a small suitcase for my things. After I packed, I climbed into bed and closed my eyes, but I knew sleep was out of the question. I watched the light against the ceiling fade from ashy grey, to dark smoke, to pitch black.

The following afternoon, Mario took a taxi and met me at the Malgrins. I watched him walk toward the front door carrying the suitcase that he and I had shared when we left Cuba four years before. We sat on the sofa and waited for Mr. Ramos to arrive. For a split second, I thought it might have all been a hoax, but then I heard Mr. Ramos's car pull into the driveway. Mr. Malgrin carried my suitcase to the car with Mrs. Malgrin in tow. After he placed it in the trunk, they both shook my hand.

"Good luck to you, Catalina."

"Thank you, both."

They turned and walked back up to the house and stood on the porch. Mario and I got in the car. As Mr. Ramos backed out of the driveway and drove off, I turned back to see Mr. and Mrs. Malgrin waving.

We drove to the airport, and Mr. Ramos parked the car. We walked to the Delta ticket counter to check in, and Mr. Ramos handed us our tickets. I rubbed the ticket in my hand. Mr. Ramos walked us to our gate.

"This is it," he said.

"Thank you," I said. "For everything."

"It was my pleasure. Take good care, now."

No sooner had he turned to go than the woman behind the counter announced that our flight was boarding. It was June 1st, and Mario and I boarded the plane nearly four years to the day that we had left Cuba. I sat beside Mario by the window. After the plane took off and soared into the cloudless sky, the stewardess handed me and Mario cocktail napkins. I ordered a coke. The bubbles fizzled my nose. The sun was setting, but I could still make out the faint shadows of mountains and slivers of rivers until finally the bright sun blew out. And there was only darkness and my reflection in the window. I smiled at myself. My breath fogged up the glass, and I drew a heart.

As we flew high above the ground, I thought of my girlfriends down there somewhere and hoped they'd all find happiness. Years later, Nené helped me track down some of the girls from the orphanage. I never found out what had happened to Martha and Paulette Cadre.

We learned that not long after Maria and Frances joined their parents in Miami, their father was murdered—shot to death by a thug trying to rob him.

I was always sorry that I didn't get a chance to go to Elaine Lugo's wedding. She was so happy, and I was happy for her. She was out of the orphanage and had started her brand new life. Not long after she and Nelson were married, the police stopped them in their driveway. They had just come home from dinner. The police accused Nelson of taking and dealing drugs, which of course, was untrue. When he tried to tell them that they had made a mistake and got the wrong man, they understood his arguing as aggressive, dangerous behavior. They pulled out their guns and shot him dead right there in his driveway, right in front of Elaine. The two policemen were charged with murder, but an all-white jury found them innocent, and they were set free.

Vivian ended up staying in New Orleans. Like Maria and Frances' father, Vivian's father was also shot to death. Some men had broken into their home, and he had caught them in the act, so they killed him. Vivian eventually married again, had a few children, and became a teacher. Years later when I learned that Vivian's mother passed away, I tried to contact her to give her my condolences, but she never responded. I don't blame her. Sometimes it best to leave the past in the past.

As the sun sank slowly, the sky turned a bright orange then faded to a deep indigo blue. The ground below was pitch black, but I could see a faint glow on the horizon before us.

"This is the Captain speaking. We'll be starting our descent into JFK. Stewardesses, please prepare the cabin for landing."

The flight attendants made one more round through the cabin gathering cups and papers and checking that trays were up and locked. I had heard that on my father's death bed, he had made Pete promise that he would take good care of me and Mario. Pete kept his promise and then some. He had gathered the whole family back together. We left Cuba in stages: me and Mario in 1962, then Pete by way of the Uruguay Embassy and through Mexico, then years later, the rest of the family.

Life takes you places you never imagined. We drift from mystery to mystery finding some doors closed and some windows open. It's a map with a thousand folds. I realized that I am part of a larger arc comprised of peace and goodness and suffering and injustice. It was here long before me, and my children will be a part of it, too.

About my time in New Orleans, I was shown great heartache, but I was blessed with happiness, too. Funny thing about happiness, most of the time while its happening, it slips right by you without you even feeling its presence. It's only realized later in the throb of a memory, where it remains. You can either choose to relive it again in that memory place or forget it and feel nothing at all.

As we drew closer to New York City, I saw the glow of the city lights brighten the horizon like the sun rising on a fresh new day. My insides warmed, and I felt welcomed. I was going to a city that was big and diverse and inclusive. I was finally going to be with my family again. The city lights seemed to stretch out in front of the plane for miles and miles. They shimmered like sunlight glittering off the waves of the ocean, rolling out into a world that was entirely new.

THE END

ACKNOWLEDGEMENTS

I am eternally grateful for Gladys Dubovsky—for her friendship, love, and encouragement. And finally, to my sister, Patty Collins, for her unwavering love and support.

ABOUT THE AUTHOR

Debbie has an MFA in creative writing from Florida International University. She has written two other books: *The Fisherman,* a novel set during the Prohibition, and *W.H. Auden, Poetry, and Me: A 102-year-old reluctant poet reflects on life, poetry, and her famous teacher.* She lives in Upstate New York.

ENDNOTES

1   Dolgoff, Sam. "The Cuban Revolution A Critical Perspective: The Batista Era." *Anarchy Archives*. http://dwardmac.pitzer.edu/Anarchist_Archives/bright/dolgoff/cubanrevolution/chapter6.html

2   Lazo, Mario. *Dagger in the Heart: American Policy Failures in Cuba*. (New York, NY: Funk & Wagnalls, a Division of Reader's Digest Books, Inc., 1968), 73-75. http://www.latinamericanstudies.org/book/Dagger-in-the-Heart.pdf.

3   Ibid.

4   Schepers, Emile. "Movement the changed the world began in Cuba July 26, 1953." *People's World*. July 24, 2014. http://www.peoplesworld.org/article/movement-that-changed-the-world-began-in-cuba-july-26-195/

5   De la Cova, Antonio Rafael. *The Moncada Attack: Birth of the Cuban Revolution*. (Columbia, SC: University of South Carolina Press, 2007), 37.

6   "Fidel's Favorite Book and Why You Should Read It." *teleSUR*. November 23, 2017. https://www.telesurtv.net/english/news/Fidels-Favourite-Book-and-Why-You-Should-Read-It-20161202-0022.html

7   Editor of History. "1959 Castro sworn in." *History, This Day in History*. https://www.history.com/this-day-in-history/castro-sworn-in

8   Sierra, J.A. "The Landing of the Granma." *historyofcuba*. http://www.historyofcuba.com/history/granma.htm

9   Shapiro, Samuel. Invisible Latin America. (North Stratford, NH: Ayer Company Publishing, Inc., 1963), 77.

10 "Fulgencio Batista" *Real Life Villains Wiki*. http://real-life-villains.wikia.com/wiki/Fulgencio_Batista

11 "Recalling Castro's Ascension—And CIA Reaction." *NPR Morning Edition*. January 1, 2009. https://www.npr.org/templates/story/story.php?storyId=98921086

12 "Just Like Jesus, Fidel Castro Also Had a Dove Descend From Heaven and Land on His Shoulder." *Facts About Religion*. https://factsaboutreligion.wordpress.com/2015/01/21/just-like-jesus-fidel-castro-also-had-a-dove-descend-from-heaven-and-land-on-his-shoulder/

13   "Murdered by ché: The true face of a terrorist mass murdered, by the Young America's Foundation." *TheRealCuba.com*. http://www.therealcuba.com/?page_id=32

14   Wilkinson, Cassandra. "The bitter truth about Che Guevara." *The Australian*. July 14, 2007. https://www.theaustralian.com.au/opinion/the-bitter-truth-about-che-guevara/news-story/4bb4734c33468e1f49a329d6889d6db1?sv=1ad8ac8f-1f46900ec4c2d69a3da21f4b

15   Ibid.

16   Seelie, Tod. "Inside an Abandoned Panopticon Prison in Cuba: The striking Presidio Modelo once house Fidel Castro." Atlas Obscura. June 19, 2017. https://www.atlasobscura.com/articles/panopticon-prison-cuba

17   Gamez Torres, Nora. "Uncovering a dark secret at 'Model Prison'." *The Miami Herald*. October 26, 2014. http://www.miamiherald.com/news/nation-world/world/americas/cuba/article3385936.html

18   "History: The Cuban Children's Exodus." *Operation Pedro Pan Group, Inc.* http://www.pedropan.org/category/history
19   "Kindertransport, 1938-1940." *Holocaust Encyclopedia*. https://www.ushmm.org/wlc/en/article.php?ModuleId=10005260

20   Zimmerman, Dwight Jon. "Operation Pied Piper: The Evacuation of English Children During World War II." *Defense Media Network*. December 31, 2011. https://www.defensemedianetwork.com/stories/operation-pied-piper-the-evacuation-of-english-children-during-world-war-ii/

21   Ibid.

22   Editor of The Telegraph. "'I was sure that children would not want to be told that this old lady was Lucy'." *The Telegraph*. December 2005. https://www.telegraph.co.uk/news/uknews/1505196/I-was-sure-that-children-would-not-want-to-be-told-that-this-old-lady-was-Lucy.html

23   Forbes, Jack D. *Africans and Native Americans: the language of race and the evolution of Red-Black peoples*. (Chicago, IL: University of Illinois Press, 1993), 145.

24   "How to Become a Catholic Nun." *A Nun's Life Ministry*. https://anunslife.org/how-to-become-a-nun

25   "What was Jim Crow?" *Jim Crow Museum of Racist Memorabilia at Ferris State University*. https://ferris.edu/jimcrow/what.htm

26   "The Coon Caricature." *Jim Crow Museum of Racist Memorabilia at Ferris State University*. https://ferris.edu/jimcrow/coon/

27   "Black Codes." *History*. https://www.history.com/topics/black-history/black-codes

28   "Lynching in America: Confronting the Legacy of Racial Terror." *Equal Justice Initiative*. Third Edition. https://lynchinginamerica.eji.org/report/

29   J., Renata. "Luther Holbert and Wife: Burned at Stake for Allegedly Murdering Two Men." *Black Then Discovering Our History*. March 21, 2017. https://blackthen.com/luther-holbert-wife-burned-stake-allegedly-murdering-two-men/

30   Editor of the New York Times. "A Terror That Blacks Faced, and Torture Today." *The New York Times*. December 28, 2008. https://www.nytimes.com/2008/12/29/opinion/l29lynch.html

31   "Homer Plessy Biography." *Biography*. https://www.biography.com/people/homer-plessy-21105789

32   Duplessis Jasmin, Alicia. "Remembering the desegregation of Tulane." *Tulane University New Wave*. September 30, 2014. http://www.ohr.tulane.edu/news/newwave/093014_remembering-the-desegregation-of-tulane.cfm?RenderForPrint=1

33   Suchlicki, Jaime. "Carlos Manuel de Céspedes: An excerpt from CUBA: FROM COLOMBUS TO CASTRO." *History of Cuba*. Part Two—Towards Independence. http://www.historyofcuba.com/history/cespedes.htm

34   "The Ten-Year War (1868-78)." *History of Cuba*. http://www.historyofcuba.com/history/funfacts/tenyear.htm

35   "September 8: Ochún's Feast Day in Cuba." *AboutSanteria*. http://www.aboutsanteria.com/la-virgen-de-la-caridad-de-cobre.html

36   "Emmett Till." *Biography*. https://www.biography.com/people/emmett-till-507515

37   Duncan, Timothyna. "EXCLUSIVE - 'She's trying to find a way to go to heaven': Rage of Emmett Till's family after white housewife who accused him of sexual threat 62 years ago so husband who lynched him would be cleared admits she lied." *The Daily Mail*. January 31, 2017. http://www.dailymail.co.uk/news/article-4176582/Emmett-Till-s-family-upset-Carolyn-Bryant-confession.html

38   Pérez-Peña, Richard. "Woman Linked to 1955 Emmett Till Murder Tells Historian Her Claims Were False." *The New York Times*. January 27, 2017. https://www.nytimes.com/2017/01/27/us/emmett-till-lynching-carolyn-bryant-donham.html

39   Joiner, Lottie L. "How the Children of Birmingham Changed the Civil Rights Movement." *The Daily Beast*. May 2, 2013. https://www.thedailybeast.com/how-the-children-of-birmingham-changed-the-civil-rights-movement

40   Ellis, Glenn. "Remembering my four friends 50 years later." *Kids in Birmingham 1963*. http://kidsinbirmingham1963.org/remembering-my-four-friends-50-years-later/

41   Editor of the Twin Cities Pioneer Press. "Pastor at famed Birmingham church dies." *Twin Cities Pioneer Press*. November 19, 2007. https://www.twincities.com/2007/11/19/pastor-at-famed-birmingham-church-dies/

42   "Greensboro Sit-In." *History*. https://www.history.com/topics/black-history/the-greensboro-sit-in

43   Grunfeld, David. "Woolworth's store in New Orleans is demolished, site of the 1960 first locally organized lunch counter sit-in." *The Times-Picayune*. February 26, 2015. http://www.nola.com/politics/index.ssf/2015/02/woolworths_store_in_new_orlean.html

44   Shah, Khushbu. "50 Years Ago the Supreme Court Ended Segregation in Restaurants: It was a tough pill for some Southern restaurant to swallow." *Eater*. December 15, 2014. https://www.eater.com/2014/12/15/7393917/50-years-ago-supreme-court-ended-segregation-restaurants

45   "Storm That Drowned a City: A 300-Year Struggle." WSKG Nova. http://www.pbs.org/wgbh/nova/orleans/struggle.html

46   Swenson, Dan. "Saenger Theatre milestones from its opening in 1927 to its renovation in 2013." The Times-Picayune. September 26, 2013. http://www.nola.com/arts/index.ssf/2013/09/saenger_theatre_milestones_fro.html

47   Ibid.

www.ingramcontent.com/pod-product-compliance
Lightning Source LLC
Chambersburg PA
CBHW052055110526
44591CB00013B/2220